C000244648

THE ARCHAEOLOGY OF TIME

It might seem obvious that time lies at the heart of archaeology since archaeology is about the past. However, the issue of time is complicated and often problematic, and although we take it very much for granted, our understanding of time affects the way we do archaeology.

This book is an introduction not just to the issues of chronology and dating, but to time as a theoretical concept and how this is understood and employed in contemporary archaeology. It provides a full discussion of chronology and change, time and the nature of the archaeological record, and the perception of time and history in past societies.

Drawing on a wide range of archaeological examples from a variety of regions and periods, *The Archaeology of Time* provides students with a crucial source book on one of the key themes of archaeology.

Gavin Lucas is Assistant Director of the Institute of Archaeology in Reykjavik. He is the author of *Critical Approaches to Fieldwork* (2001) and co-editor with Victor Buchli of *Archaeologies of the Contemporary Past* (2001).

THEMES IN ARCHAEOLOGY
Edited by Julian Thomas
University of Manchester

THE ARCHAEOLOGY OF PERSONHOOD
An anthropological approach
Chris Fowler

ARCHAEOLOGY, RITUAL, RELIGION
Timothy Insoll

THE ARCHAEOLOGY OF TIME
Gavin Lucas

THE ARCHAEOLOGY
OF TIME

Gavin Lucas

LONDON AND NEW YORK

First published 2005
by Routledge
2 Park Square, Milton Park, Abingdon, Oxon OX14 4RN

Simultaneously published in the USA and Canada
by Routledge
270 Madison Ave, New York, NY 10016

Routledge is an imprint of the Taylor & Francis Group

© 2005 Gavin Lucas

Typeset in Garamond by
Florence Production Ltd, Stoodleigh, Devon
Printed and bound in Great Britain by
TJ International, Padstow, Cornwall

All rights reserved. No part of this book may
be reprinted or reproduced or utilized in any form or by any
electronic, mechanical, or other means, now known or hereafter
invented, including photocopying and recording, or in
any information storage or retrieval system, without
permission in writing from the publishers.

British Library Cataloguing in Publication Data
A catalogue record for this book is available from the British Library

Library of Congress Cataloging in Publication Data
Lucas, Gavin, 1965–
The archaeology of time/Gavin Lucas.
p. cm. – (Themes in archaeology)
Includes bibliographical references and index.
1. Archaeology. 2. Time. I. Title. II. Series.
CC75. 7.L83 2005
930.1–dc22   2004009689

ISBN 0–415–31197–7 (hbk)
ISBN 0–415–31198–5 (pbk)

CONTENTS

ILLUSTRATIONS

Figures

Tables

PREFACE

This is a book I should have written many years ago. My doctoral thesis largely focused on the concept of time in archaeology, which I worked through with material from the Neolithic and Bronze Age of eastern Yorkshire in northern England. Yet, looking back, it has been nearly ten years since that was completed and I have published next to nothing on the concept of time – except one short paper in a non-archaeological journal (Lucas 1997). Part of the reason for this lies in the fact that soon after my PhD, I moved into a very different area of archaeological research; it was only when Julian Thomas suggested I write a short book on time for the Routledge series 'Themes in Archaeology' that I decided to use the opportunity to return to this early interest. This book inevitably draws heavily on the research and reading I did for my doctoral thesis, but in no way is it a published version of that thesis; it is a completely different and new piece of work which particularly – and extensively – draws on the massive increase in publications on time in archaeology since my thesis was written, as well as developments in my own thoughts on the subject. Indeed, in many ways, waiting ten years has produced a much better book; if I had written this book back then, it would have suffered from lack of case studies and examples, as well as breadth and diversity of investigation.

The writing of this book has benefited from a number of people who are warmly thanked here. First, to Julian Thomas who initiated the project, and to several anonymous reviewers who saw the synopsis – all these helped to shape the general structure of the book. Second, to those who kindly read and commented on the draft manuscript – they provided much-needed critical distance as well as support that it was going in the right direction. In this regard, I would like to thank Kevin Greene, Cornelius Holtorf, Tim Murray and Michael Shanks – even where we disagreed on some points, their input has been invaluable. Final thanks must go to Richard Stoneman and Celia Tedd of Routledge for facilitating the whole production process so smoothly and with such commitment.

All figures (except 2.3, 2.5 and 4.2) were produced by the author, though some have been adapted from original sources; these sources are acknowledged in the captions. The author thanks Oscar Aldred for his landscape representation models (Figure 2.3), Cornelius Holtorf for his non-linear chronology diagram (Figure 2.5) and Andrew Hall for his drawing of jar 3732 (Figure 4.2).

This is a short book, intended as an introduction to the concept of time in archaeology – I have tried to cover a broad range of themes and perspectives while still retaining some overall coherence. Indeed, though intended as a general introduction, my personal stamp remains present, in both the style and nature of the argument – it could not be otherwise. I have also tried to make the subject of time and debates around it as accessible as possible, but inevitably some portions will be harder going than others. For all this, I hope most readers will find this book informative, if not provocative.

1

BEYOND CHRONOLOGY

Introduction: why should archaeologists think about time?

Why is time important to archaeology – indeed, why should anyone write a whole book about the subject or, for that matter, read one? As Stuart Piggot once wrote, 'Any enquiry into the past which does not reckon with the dimension of time is obviously nonsense' (Piggott 1959: 51). It might seem obvious that time is important to archaeology simply because archaeology is about the past; it is a historical science or discipline. On that recognition, then, a book about time is not only reasonable but essential. Yet, on further reflection, one might also ask, how much is there to actually say about time? Most archaeologists, when asked about time, might think about dating and chronology and, indeed, this is perhaps what first springs to mind. Certainly, issues of dating have been, and will continue to be, of major concern to archaeologists but since this is not a book about dating techniques – and my apologies to the reader who opened this book thinking it was – what is left to say? Well, quite a lot actually. What I can at least say, in anticipation, is that this book aims to explore time as a theoretical concept and how this is understood and employed in contemporary archaeology. For it is precisely because time lies at the heart of archaeology that we may take it too much for granted, and fail to see the ways in which time, in particular the way we understand time, affects the way we do archaeology.

1

The presumption here, one that is no stranger to philosophical and social theory, is that time is not a straightforward concept but, in fact, it is extremely problematic.

In this first chapter, I want to examine the taken-for-granted assumptions we have about time in archaeology, in particular how this is expressed through the central concept of chronology. But more than that, I also want to argue that the conception of time that underlies chronology is a limiting one, especially when we see that it has also influenced the nature of archaeological interpretations of culture change and prehistory. Time and change are close bedfellows – they are so related as concepts that, perhaps, it is hard to think of them apart. Indeed, as this chapter will try to explain, the restrictive conception of time in chronology is precisely problematic because it does not really engage with this relation, and this sustains a context for very impoverished interpretations of cultural change. At the end of the chapter, I briefly review the literature of archaeological discussion on time, which is small but growing; theoretical discussion of the concept has only emerged in the last 15 years, but already some broad fields of research and direction have been established and these will form the basis of the next two chapters. Chapter 4 uses a case study to explore these issues in more detail and the final chapter will summarize the themes of this book as well as look forward to new directions in which the discussion of time in archaeology might lead.

Chronology and archaeological time

How do archaeologists traditionally conceive of time? Perhaps the easiest way to answer this is to consider the phrases employed to denote time in archaeology. For example:

- The Holocene started $c.10,000$ years BP.
- Food vessels are a feature of the Bronze Age.
- The Roman town has origins in the Claudio-Neronian period.
- This structure belongs to Phase IIb.
- This well has a *terminus post quem* of AD 330.
- This layer is earlier than that pit.

All these examples express basically the same conception of time – as *chronology*. Chronology, according to the OED, is the 'science of computing dates', and all the different terms or phrases highlighted in the examples refer to different dating systems or chronologies that archaeologists have constructed over the history of its discipline. Different chronologies are used for different contexts – for example, Bronze Age refers to the Three Age System devised for prehistoric Europe by Thomsen in the nineteenth century, while 10,000 years BP refers to radiocarbon dating established only in the 1950s. Each of the examples – and there could have been many more – refer to chronologies of varying applicability, from site specific (e.g. Phase IIb) to universal (e.g. AD 330). Some chronologies have been short-lived and some terms are no longer generally used (e.g. eneolithic) while some have had lasting impact, especially the Three Age System. Some are specific to archaeology (e.g. Bronze Age) while some derive from other disciplines such as geology (Holocene) or Classics (Claudio-Neronian). The key axis that differentiates all archaeological chronologies, however, is the distinction between *absolute* and *relative* chronologies.

By an absolute chronology, is meant a chronology based on a time framework that is *independent* of the data being studied – typically, this is expressed through the calendrical system, with dates in years AD/BC or BP. The first and fifth examples given above use absolute chronologies. In contrast, a relative chronology is one based on the inter-dependence of the data being studied – this can be anything from stratigraphy to periodization. Here, the chronology of the data is solely expressed relative to other data – all the examples except the fifth contain a reference to a relative chronology. Relative chronologies are the oldest in archaeology and, before the advent of scientific dating techniques (see below), they provided the only means of constructing chronologies. Relative chronologies can be divided into two main types: primary and secondary. The primary chronologies are chiefly systems for working out relative sequences of archaeological deposits and artefacts through the principles of stratigraphy (Harris 1989), seriation (Marquardt 1978) and typology (Gräslund 1987). These basic methods were used to construct larger, secondary chronological

3

systems by collating several such relative sequences together; the Three Age System in Europe is the classic example of a secondary or derived chronological system. All periodizations are relative chronologies and while most archaeological periodizations are based on the collation of primary systems, a few are drawn from other disciplines such as geological/environmental periods or historical periods.

Absolute dating in the form of a calendrical system of years has always been recognized in archaeology, but the only way of using it, until recently, was through association with historical records. This meant either linking a site to a historical event through some continuity or correlation – or having an archaeological find that has a date on it (e.g. a coin) or some other reference to a dated event (e.g. inscription). Such dates need to be treated with caution, of course, because of problems of re-use and not conflating the date of the object with the date of its deposition. Historical dating, whether through associative or intrinsic features, is fine when there are historical records, but for most of prehistory, this is lacking – indeed, this is one definition of the term 'prehistory'. The development of scientific techniques for providing absolute dates only emerged in the 1950s as the archaeological applications of radioactive decay were realized, of which the most well-known is radiocarbon or C14 (Zeuner 1946). Since then, there has been an ever-expanding range of scientific dating techniques (e.g. thermoluminescence, electro-spin resonance, amino acid racemization), almost all of which provide an independent, and therefore absolute, dating method (Aitken 1990). In fact, ironically, radiocarbon dating, at least in so far as it is expressed in a calibrated form, is properly a relative system, since it is cross-referenced to another chronology – dendrochronology. Nevertheless, in principle it is fair to group it with absolute chronologies. Table 1.1 summarizes the principal different archaeological chronologies.

Most relative chronologies can be, and are, tied in to absolute chronologies, especially the secondary chronologies, though this has not always been easy. In the case of Roman periodizations based on imperial reigns (e.g. Claudio-Neronian), there are historical records to provide links to our calendrical system, but in the

Table 1.1 Main types of relative and absolute chronologies

Relative chronologies	*Absolute chronologies*
Primary	*Historical*
Stratigraphy	Associative
Seriation	Intrinsic
Typology	
Secondary	*Scientific*
Periodization	Radiocarbon
	Dendrochronology
	Etc.

case of prehistoric periodizations such as the Three Age System, this has been a far more difficult endeavour which only the advent of radiocarbon dating has put on a sure footing (Renfrew 1978). The original method was a technique called *cross-dating* which drew on historical records left by the 'great civilizations' in Egypt and Mesopotamia (Figure 1.1). One of the earliest attempts was Worsaae's chronological table published in 1878. However, it was Flinders Petrie who did most to promote this method of cross-dating using the Egyptian records. Using dated Egyptian imports found in Greek contexts and Greek imports found in dated Egyptian contexts enabled him to provide an absolute chronology for the Greek Bronze Age. Extending this method beyond south-eastern Europe, however, proved more of a challenge as imports became increasingly rare the further north and west one moved. Montelius was the first to attempt a more sophisticated link between absolute and relative chronologies for North-west Europe, but it was Childe who took it to its full conclusion.

Extending the chronology involved creating a series of relative chronologies that could be first knitted together, and then, eventually, tied into the absolute chronologies available for the Near East. Montelius made a start knitting together regional chronologies for Western Europe, but it took Childe's breadth of vision to create the pan-European synthesis needed to create the links to the Aegean and Near East (Burkitt and Childe 1932). However, Childe's synthesis has not stood the test of time, as he himself

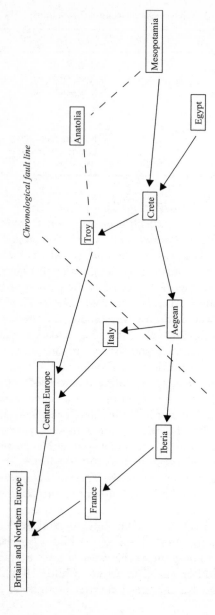

Figure 1.1 Links in cross-dating between the Near East and North-west Europe.
Source: Adapted from Renfrew 1978.

started to realize just before his death (Childe 1957). Not only were some of the assumptions in his diffusionary argument spurious (especially the idea that cultural innovation always spread from south/east to north/west), but they were shown to be wrong by the application of new scientific dating, namely radiocarbon.

However, the development of scientific dating techniques does need to be contextualized and not simply seen as a simple story of scientific progress. While it is true that the various attempts to fix relative chronologies to an absolute one began as far back as the late nineteenth century, it was only with the shift in the focus of the archaeological concept of culture from a universal idea (Culture with a capital 'C') to a regional conception (culture-group) in the 1920s that the question of absolute chronology became more urgent (Trigger 1989; Lucas 1997). This is because under the universal concept of culture, all that really mattered was how any regional chronology fitted into the universal model of culture change – evolutionism. But once interest shifted towards regional culture histories, regional chronologies only provided a circular method of dating such histories and, thus, an absolute chronology became much more important. In this sense, it could be argued that it was Childe's very synthesis that made the radiocarbon revolution happen – if his transformation of the archaeological concept of culture and prehistory had not happened, perhaps there would not have been the drive to provide an absolute chronology or recognize the value of radioactive decay as a dating tool in the first place (Lucas 1997).

This shift comes out very clearly when we compare two quotes, one from Flinders Petrie in 1899 and the other from Mortimer Wheeler half a century later:

> [T]he main value of dates is to show the sequence of events; and it would matter very little if the time from Augustus to Constantine had occupied six centuries instead of three, or if Alexander had lived only two centuries before Augustus. The order of events and the relation of one country to another is the main essential in history. Indeed, the tacit common-sense of historians

> agrees in treating the periods of great activity and production more fully than the arid ages of barbarism, and so substituting practically a scale of activity as the standard rather than a scale of years.
>
> (Petrie 1899: 295)

> First, without an absolute chronology cultures of different regions cannot be assessed: in other words, the vital causative factors of human 'progress' cannot be authoritatively reconstructed, and may be widely misunderstood. Secondly, the fluctuating tempo of human achievement – cannot be estimated: the lightning flash, for example, of Periclean Athens, or the glow of the slow-moving riverine civilizations.
>
> (Wheeler 1954: 39)

Although I have maintained a distinction throughout this section between absolute and relative chronology, not all archaeologists would necessarily agree with this characterization (Colman *et al.* 1987; Ramenofsky 1998). Within post-Newtonian physics, time is, of course, regarded as relative rather than absolute. Indeed, in many ways, the distinction between absolute and relative time is mostly one of scale and regularity. All chronologies are ultimately based on events that incorporate time into their very structure – the planetary cycle (i.e. calendrical chronology), radiocarbon decay, tree ring growth, stratification or typological change; some are just based on smaller and more regular time units than others. Thus, Ann Ramenofsky has suggested that rather than use the distinction between relative and absolute chronologies, there should be a distinction between chronologies based simply on ordinal systems against those that also incorporate an interval system (Ramenofsky 1998: 79–80). Most of what, conventionally, we call relative chronologies, are ordinal systems – that is, chronologies that have direction but units of non-specific duration – while interval systems, usually absolute chronologies, do have units of specific and equal duration.

In many ways, this may seem like a semantic distinction – since we all understand what we mean by relative and absolute chronologies, perhaps we should just stick with these terms. Perhaps. Nonetheless, the question of scale and regularity that generally distinguishes the two *is* an important issue that should not be forgotten, because it ties into the question of interpreting change. We might think that, as archaeologists, our chief problem when it comes to time is refining our chronologies – it seems intuitive that controlling time is *the* major temporal issue in archaeology. Yet this is misleading, for the level of chronological resolution is directly related to the nature of the interpretation we need to make. I discuss this issue more in the next chapter, but the key point is how our chronologies perform relative to the requirements of the interpretation – a relative or ordinal chronology might be sufficient in many cases, but in others a more absolute or interval chronology would be better. But, here, the dichotomy becomes obstructive, since it is more of a spectrum of techniques rather than a dichotomy; indeed, the dichotomy may only serve to confuse issues. For example, Ramenofsky argues that the debates surrounding the dating of the first humans in North America at Meadowcroft Rockshelter is largely a product of conflict between two systems – the ordinal system of periodization and the interval system of radiometric dates (ibid.: 81–2). The problem at this site is that the radiometric dates give a time that suggests late Pleistocene, while all the artefactual and ecofactual evidence points to a Holocene date. From one perspective, the radiometric dates must be wrong, while from another, the supposed Holocene/Pleistocene boundary may be wrong. This is an irresolvable problem, because it is not an empirical issue but a conceptual one, a clash of two chronological systems.

Chronology and universal time

Archaeologists today take for granted the role of chronologies in the discipline and there is no doubt they form an essential part of archaeological reasoning. But in this section I want to raise some question marks over it, in particular, how chronology affects the nature of archaeological interpretation of the past. I will suggest that chronology – whether relative or absolute – is theoretically problematic and for one chief reason: it presents time as a uniform, linear phenomenon which has tended to define the model for historical explanation in a similar uniform, linear way. Before I delve into the theory of this, it would be useful to map out the problem in terms of archaeological research and frameworks.

To begin with, it is useful to ask what it is that relative and absolute (or ordinal and interval) chronologies share in common. Consider Figure 1.2 – it shows a fairly common temporal chart with a periodization of Egyptian dynastic chronology (relative) in one column and a calendrical dateline (absolute) in the other. Two characteristics are similar in both systems: their linear order and their divisibility into exclusive units. Both the periodization and the calendar flow in one direction and each is divided into discrete, non-overlapping units, i.e. periods or years. The main difference is that periodization uses much larger units than the calendrical system but, in principle, they share the same structure. In short, they presume a specific conception of time as a uni-linear sequence or series.

Given this very specific concept of time underlying chronology, how does this affect the way archaeology traditionally conceives of cultural change? In many ways, the Three Age System in the late nineteenth century was more than a periodization; it also contained explanatory potential. In particular, it carried very definite evolutionary implications which have been mostly lost or greatly diluted today. The evolutionary ideals that underlay the Three Age System was famously articulated by scholars such as Lubbock in *Prehistoric Times* (1865), but evolution as a general theory of history was presented in most detail by Morgan in *Ancient Society* (1877). He grouped societies and the general course of human history into three basic stages: savagery, barbarism and civilization. Of course, it was recognized that history did not proceed uniformly everywhere; indeed, it was precisely the presence of 'other' societies contemporary with nineteenth-century Europe that provided the basis of this model. The usual term for these societies was 'survivals', i.e. remnants of a past age, who had

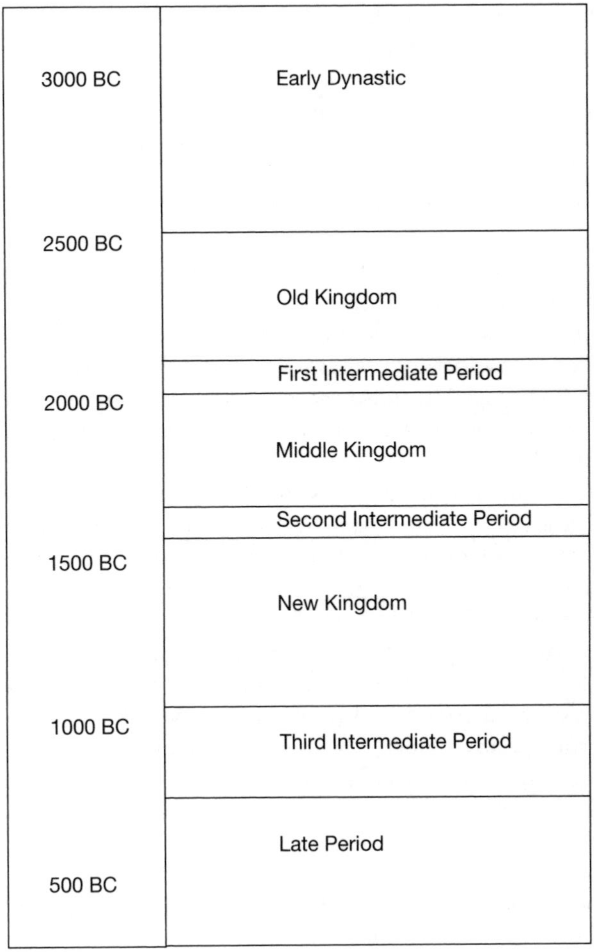

3000 BC	Early Dynastic
2500 BC	Old Kingdom
	First Intermediate Period
2000 BC	Middle Kingdom
	Second Intermediate Period
1500 BC	New Kingdom
1000 BC	Third Intermediate Period
500 BC	Late Period

Figure 1.2 Egyptian dynastic chronology with conventional
calendar dates.

not progressed beyond savagery or barbarism. Some scholars also argued that some societies might regress as much as progress, so that evolutionism was not necessarily one directional – past civilizations may have descended back into barbarism for example. In the early twentieth century, this same scheme was still adhered to, despite changing notions of the concept of culture as discussed above. In fact, it was Gordon Childe, the major exponent of the new cultural archaeology, who promoted the same broad evolutionary stages, with some modifications, in his most general works such as *Social Evolution* (1951) or *What Happened in History* (1942).

Morgan's original work greatly influenced Marxist theory, especially Engels who drew on *Ancient Society* in his *The Origin of the Family: Private Property and the State*, and Childe, in turn, was greatly influenced by Marxism in his re-interpretation of Morgan's evolutionary scheme. His ideas of an agricultural revolution and the urban revolution, which play key roles in his discussion of prehistory, link major changes in the nature of economic production in prehistoric societies to Morgan's evolutionary stages and the Three Age System (Childe 1935). Although Childe's scheme has largely been dropped today, many of his ideas remain, particularly his conceptualization of the agricultural and urban revolutions. In the 1950s, new evolutionary ideas emerged from North America, partly influenced by Childe's views, and these crystallized in the 1960s with Sahlins and Service's four-stage evolutionary schema based primarily on the complexity of social structure: Bands, Tribes, Chiefdoms and States (Sahlins and Service 1960). These evolutionary stages through which human societies passed were explicitly distinguished from the actual course of history for any particular society or region. The terms general and specific evolution were coined to underline the fact that societies could regress as much as progress, and develop at different rates and through different causal mechanisms. This neo-evolutionary model is the one still in use today, albeit modified (e.g. Johnson and Earle 1987), and remains the dominant paradigm of social change in the US and, to a lesser extent, in Europe.

Both the early and later evolutionary schemes share a typological model of history and present history, ultimately as a uniform, linear phenomenon (Lucas 2001: 132; McGuire 1992: 155). Even recognizing that societies may regress as well as progress, and develop at quite different rates – and both old and new evolutionary theories did recognize this, either implicitly or explicitly – ultimately, the model still presents a universal view of history. All societies and all of human history can be encompassed with this simple typological scheme of three or four stages, which are mutually exclusive and are arranged in a linear, uni-directional sequence. It does not matter that the actual course of history can go back as well as forward, the *conceptual* order is uni-directional – towards increasing complexity in the case of Band to State, or increasing humanity/culture in the case of savagery to civilization. And, on the whole, the actual course of prehistory is, more often than not, presented as following this conceptual order.

It is not hard to see how similar the temporal structure of evolutionary theory is to chronology (relative or absolute): both share the same notion of a directional, linear view of time divided into discrete units (Table 1.2). Not only evolutionism but many archaeological narratives share this same structure, narratives that sustain a certain model of explanation called *totalizing*, which is sustained through a specific conception of time as expressed in chronology. Julian Thomas has criticized this attitude of totalization with respect to discourses on the Neolithic, and the search for its defining characteristics (Thomas 1994); but how is the concept of time implicated in such narratives? Here, the critique by the Marxist historian Althusser is revealing; in his book *For Marx*, Althusser problematized the concept of history by addressing its presuppositions about time (Althusser 1969). He argued that by asserting a single temporality (i.e. chronology) in which all history takes place, historical interpretation ultimately seeks totality and closure. Because chronology presents time as a universal and homogeneous field in which events take place, historians tend to assume that history, itself, unfolds in a like manner. As time is homogeneous and universal so, ultimately, is history. Against this, Althusser suggests that there is no single continuous time, or universal time frame or reference but, rather, different temporalities, which produce different histories. Cultural evolution is the obvious exemplar of this kind of totalizing history but, more generally, Althusser suggests that any kind of history that attempts to be universal in its coverage, such as a periodization, reproduces the same assumption about time. Such an approach has also been linked to the politics of European hegemony in colonial contexts and writing about the 'other' (Young 1990).

Many archaeologists may find a totalizing narrative reassuring, or have no problem with it. However, there is a very important issue here about constructing stories of the past; for much of archaeology's history, there have been grand narratives that attempt to survey the development of human culture in totality during prehistory – these need not always take the systematic form of social evolution, but address global cultural developments such as the agricultural or urban revolutions (e.g. see Sherratt 1995). Many contemporary archaeological studies avoid these grand narratives, yet, at the same time, they give a coherence to archaeology as a discipline. Ultimately, what is at stake here is the Enlightenment vision of a total history, archaeology as a science of humanity where the whole of human history can be embraced within a single vision, a single chronology (see also Chapter 5). However one feels about this issue, though, it is important to state that the conception of time that underlies archaeological chronology, and also grand archaeological narratives of prehistory, is a restricted one. This is not to argue that archaeology should abandon this conception of time or chronology, but to retain it as the dominant conception in our understanding of the past, only

Table 1.2 The temporal structure of chronology and evolutionism

Temporal structure	Direction	Units
Absolute chronology	Past to future	Years
Relative chronology	Stone to Iron	Periods
Evolutionism	Simple to complex	Stages

impoverishes that understanding. There have been alternative approaches to prehistory that draw on a very different conception of time and I would like to discuss these briefly and show how they differ.

Timescales and non-linear systems in archaeology

One of the earliest attempts to look at non-linear change was a study of changes in female fashion by Richardson and Kroeber in the 1940s (Richardson and Kroeber 1952). Studying qualities such as the length of the dress, they identified periodicities and cycles in a highly detailed and quantitative manner. However, this was never really developed theoretically. Since the late 1980s, however, there have been two new approaches to the notion of historical explanation that employ a different temporal structure to a simple linear process. Although inspired from quite different sources, they do share the basic idea that different historical phenomena or processes work at different temporal scales. One approach borrows from French historical theory developed by the *Annales* school, the other from post-Newtonian science and non-linear dynamics. The *Annales* school was founded in 1929 by Febvre and Bloch, but its most famous exponent, and the chief source for archaeology, has been the writings of Braudel (Braudel 1972, 1980). The *Annales* school was very critical of traditional history, by which it meant history written as a simple sequence of events; in particular, it tried to problematize the duality of history as both continuity and change (e.g. Bloch 1954). Braudel's answer to this involved distinguishing three specific timescales over which history unfolded: the long, medium and short term. The long term, or *longue durée*, covered very slow-moving processes such as the environment; the medium term referred to social or structural history, such as persistent forms of social or economic organization; and, finally, the short term referred to events or individuals, usually the main focus of most traditional history. For Braudel, each scale affected the course of the others and all were intertwined, although many have seen his main focus being on the long term. Certainly, for archaeologists, this was, initially, the most attractive given the timescales and chronological resolution available to archaeology.

Sustained interest in *Annales* theory in archaeology emerged in the late 1980s and early 1990s with the publication of several volumes variously drawing inspiration from this school (Hodder 1987; Gurevich 1995; Last 1995; Bintliff 1991; Knapp 1992). For example, in a study of change in the Midwestern United States between 3000 BC and AD 1400, Charles Cobb identified two scales of change: a long-term structure of an expanding horticultural economy and shorter-term cycles of trade (Cobb 1991). Cobb starts by identifying fluctuations in inter-regional exchange that correspond with the conventional periodization of the Late Archaic, Middle Woodland-Hopewell, and Mississippi periods. Each period is characterized by active long-distance trade which appears to stop at the juncture between each period, thus suggesting a cyclical pattern. However, above these repetitive cycles, Cobb draws out a longer-term, more general linear pattern for the whole time span, of increased agricultural production, increased social inequality and increased ritual deposition. Thus, by using two scales of analysis, Cobb is able to demonstrate both a long-term trend and fluctuations in that trend, and, as importantly, that each scale is necessary to understand the other. Thus, he argues that the increased agricultural production provided a surplus that fuelled the exchange system for the benefit of elites; however, this system was inherently unstable as neither the social organization of production, nor the trade network itself, was very coherent, and thus was prone to collapse.

Cobb's paper is of interest because it aligns itself at a general level with certain evolutionary approaches that employ non-linear models of social change. Such models argue that seeing social systems purely as static entities makes it very hard to explain change, especially sudden change and, instead, they argue that over the long term, what characterizes such systems is not so much continuity as discontinuity – instability rather than equilibrium (e.g. Renfrew and Cooke 1979; Friedman 1982). Thus, history is not a linear process but one punctuated by cycles or periods of rapid transformation. The earliest attempts to develop non-linear models of change drew on catastrophe theories developed in the natural sciences, especially the work of Thom (Thom 1975), but later approaches have taken up chaos theory and the ideas of Prigogine (Prigogine and Stengers 1984). These later approaches broaden their perspective by taking on the idea of different scales or rates of change as employed by the *Annales* school, but attempt to provide a more mathematical model of the relationship between these different scales (McGlade 1987, 1999; van der Leeuw and McGlade 1997).

This approach agrees with the *Annales* that history involves different rates of change, from geological processes to human events, and suggests that much of the discontinuity in history can be seen as the product of a conjuncture between different temporalities. Consequently, it is argued that archaeological explanations of change should alter their focus from change per se to the rate of change – and even the *changing* rate of change (Figure 1.3). Such non-linear models of social transformation use a specific model of social structures as complex systems which exhibit two key characteristics: any system *always* has a certain inbuilt instability; and this instability, though normally at low levels, will have a threshold above which, when amplified, it has the capacity to collapse or transform the system. In social systems, this instability largely comes from human agency or other idiosyncratic behaviour. In the example of exchange systems in Bronze-Age Wessex, McGlade argues that the transition from the early to later Bronze Age is characterized by such a threshold in a prestige goods economy system (McGlade 1997). He suggests that such exchange systems are inherently unstable over the long term because they are driven by individual agents; in the case of Bronze-Age Wessex, over-specialization and rigidity in the exchange network in the early period exacerbated this inherent instability to tip it over the threshold of equilibrium so that it collapsed by the late period.

Both *Annales* and non-linear approaches to social change can, perhaps, be summarized by sharing a conception of time as the tension between continuity and change. Moreover, they articulate

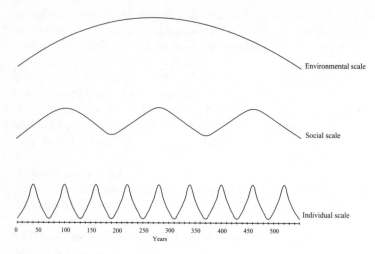

Figure 1.3 Schematic representation of different rates of change for
different processes.

this conception by reference to two basic aspects of history –
process (or the long term) and event (or the short term). How does
this conception of time differ to that which underlies chronology
and traditional evolutionary theory? As I showed earlier, the latter
generally present time as a uniform, linear sequence, and largely
one defined by continuity; consequently, the only problem was
change, for which a typological theory of evolution has been
the main solution. However, for both *Annales* and non-linear
approaches, continuity is just as much a problem as change and,
more significantly, the articulation between the two becomes
the real key issue. In different ways, each resolves this problem
by recourse to a similar model of multiple, temporal scales of
analysis. Moreover, both give greater weight to the notion of the
uniqueness of history and the particular histories of different
societies or regions, rather than promoting a universal history
such as evolution.

This is not to say that the *Annales* or non-linear approaches
abandon chronology – rather, they use a *different conception of time*

18

to chronology in constructing interpretations of prehistory, unlike Evolutionism which employs the same conception. More particularly, they seem to stress that time and event are not necessarily distinct – that time, rather than being simply an independent, homogeneous measure or container for events, is actually inextricable from events. In modern physics, especially in thermodynamics and quantum physics, this conception of time is widely accepted in contrast to the older, Newtonian idea of time as an independent dimension. Chronology is this old Newtonian time (but see Ramenofsky 1998). In many ways, this association between time and event is better problematized through the tension between continuity and change, a tension that has long been recognized in philosophical discussions of time as expressed in paradoxes such as Zeno's arrow. Let us consider the paradox of Zeno's arrow because it provides a useful way into the philosophy of time.

A brief interlude into the philosophy of time

Zeno was a Greek philosopher living in the fifth century BC and his paradox is simply this: an arrow in flight always occupies a certain point at a certain time – that is, if one were to stop the arrow at any present moment (physically, mentally or through a photograph for example), it can be said to have a fixed place at a fixed time – it is here, now (Figure 1.4). Since an arrow at rest also occupies a fixed place at a fixed time, it could be argued that the arrow in flight is *always* at rest since at any particular point in its flight it is no different from when it is at rest. Paradoxically, the arrow in flight, then, never actually moves. This paradox is based on a view of time as a succession of instants or moments – of 'nows' or 'presents'. If time is a succession of points, then the arrow 'moves' in a succession of steps; the problem is how to understand how one moment succeeds another without invoking time itself, and this is impossible for it raises the question of change, and this is exactly what Zeno's paradox questions. One is left multiplying the series of steps to infinity and succession itself being ultimately impossible. Yet, the arrow *does move*.

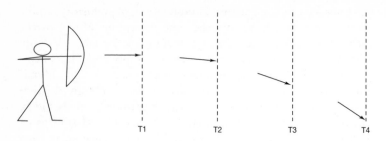

Figure 1.4 Zeno's arrow.

This fundamental paradox or *aporia* of time can be summed up by stating that any attempt to explain change will either negate it or presuppose it. And the crux of the problem lies in the fact that we cannot account for things occupying a point *and* changing; Zeno's arrow cannot both be at a certain point at a certain time, and move. Time on this model is an infinite succession of instants. Various attempts have been made to get out of this *aporia* – the fourth-century Greek philosopher Aristotle, who reports it in his *Physics* with other of Zeno's paradoxes such as Achilles and the Tortoise, refutes it on the basis that Zeno is confusing two senses of infinity – multiplicity and divisibility. Aristotle argues that time is not composed of instants, and thus the problem of infinity is a red herring – rather, time is a continuum which is infinitely divisible, which is not the same thing as infinitely multiple (Aristotle 1952).

Aristotle's discussion of time in *Physics IV*, 10–14 centres around the problem of continuity and difference from the point of view of the present moment. He discusses time in terms of movement, and thus makes it dependent on space and magnitude, defining time in terms of a duality of any present moment – that the present is both a point and a line; the present connects both past and future as a continuum, but it is also the end of the past and the beginning of the future and, thus, a punctuation (Aristotle 1952). Although on the one hand, this seems to recognize a certain aporia to time, on the other it makes time derivative of substance or spatial divisibility – time is reducible to space. It is a long leap from fourth-century BC Athens to twentieth-century AD Europe, but at the turn of the twentieth century there were two major schools which re-thought the nature of time: Anglo-American analytical philosophy and Continental phenomenology.

The British philosopher McTaggart said that there were, fundamentally, just two views on time, which he called the A series and the B series (McTaggart 1908). The A series refers to time described in terms of tense, i.e. past, present and future and emphasizes the continuous nature of time, as duration. The B series refers to time described in terms of succession, i.e. earlier than/before, later than/after, and emphasizes time as a series of point or moments. However, for the A series to make sense, it needs to be explained in terms of the B series; for example, any event cannot be both past, present and future – how does it change from one to another? To say the event *was* past, *is* present, *will be* future is to presuppose the very thing one is trying to explain; the only way out is to say that at a certain point in time it has one of these characteristics, and at another point, another. But then to use the notion of a certain point in time, presupposes the B series, so this makes the A series derivative of the B series. However, the problem with the B series is that, as a succession of points, it does not capture the flow of time which the A series contains; it does not seem to relate to experience. For example, event 'x' always comes before event 'y', regardless of our subjective view-point, i.e. whether it is past, present or future; however, to say that the relation between the two events remains the same whatever the subjective conditions, is *not* the same as saying that one event is earlier than another. The B series is not simply an order (what McTaggart calls a C series), for it has direction, and this can only derive from our subjective view of time as tensed, i.e. from past to future: the A series. For McTaggart, this problem, namely that the A series seems to be dependent on the B series and vice versa, meant that time, ultimately, must be unreal.

McTaggart's response to the paradox was based on his assumption that reality must be logical, and since time is illogical, it cannot be real. Subsequent analytical philosophy has tended to either agree with McTaggart's conclusion, or try to argue for the primacy of one series over the other (e.g. Mellor 1981). However, it is interesting to contrast this debate and attitude to developments in Continental philosophy. The French philosopher Bergson's influential paper on the division of time into its perception as duration (*durée*) and its representation as succession is, in some ways, similar to McTaggart's A and B series (Bergson 1910). Unlike McTaggart, however, Bergson relished the paradox between the two. He attempted to show how the problems of free will or Zeno's paradoxes are due to a confusion between time as *duration* and *succession*; in Zeno and Aristotle, time is seen in terms of space, that is as magnitude. Yet, Bergson argued that this is simply a representation, a convention – time is primordially not spatial (i.e. a point or a continuum), but a 'heterogeneous continuity' (Bergson 1910). In other words, Bergson is affirming an *inherently* paradoxical definition of time. Indeed, he recognizes the impossibility of giving time a logical definition, because of its pre-conceptual nature in lived experience. As soon as we represent time we betray it – this is an explicit attempt to formulate St Augustine's more poetical description of the enigmatic nature of time (Augustine 1961: ch. XI).

With Husserl, this formulation reaches an unmatched sophistication; his phenomenology of internal time-consciousness attempts to describe in detail this primordially heterogeneous continuity – what he calls the temporal flux (Husserl 1966). Husserl's study is extremely complex and it is hard to do it any justice in the small space here, so only the most general summary will be given. Following Bergson, Husserl argued that the representation of time as a succession of points is *only* a representation; that, in fact, our consciousness actually perceives time as a flux. Husserl uses the example of a musical tone – when we hear it, it *flows*, it does not consist of a series of points. The only way to actually represent that characteristic, though, is to use the representation of time as a series, but in two dimensions instead of just one. For example, the normal one-dimension model taken to represent time is as a line of successive moments, say A, B and C (Figure

1.5(a) – compare this to Zeno's arrow in Figure 1.4). In addition, however, Husserl suggests that each moment also has a depth or 'echo' (what he calls retention) which yields a second dimension if you like, say A, A′ and A″ (Figure 1.5(b)). Taken together, the flow of time is, thus, a combination of succession and retention

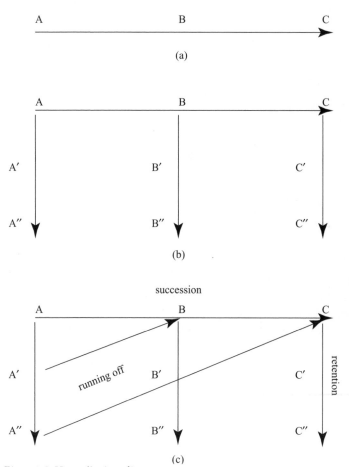

Figure 1.5 Husserl's time diagram.

which can be represented by an oblique line running off from any one moment so that any present moment is a combination of the present and previous past moments – thus C/B'/A'' (Figure 1.5(c)).

To some extent, this presentation can be criticized for being founded actually on the traditional, sequential conception of time – the two axes represent a sequence of ideal points whether of A–B–C or A–A'–A'' – and thus, ultimately, time remains derivative of a homogeneous line divisible into instants (e.g. see Ricoeur 1988: 29). However, the very fact of trying to represent a heterogeneous description of time may be inevitably entrapped within a condition of intelligibility that demands homogeneity. What is important, I think, in Husserl's account, is the way heterogeneity is evoked from homogeneity, how the 'obliqueness' of the running-off traverses and cuts up the 'straightness' of succession and retention and emphasizes the tension between the two. This describes duration without transcending it but, rather, by off-setting two potentially transcendent descriptions in a continuous dialectic. We can, perhaps, re-read Husserl's description of time as that which mediates between the line and the point, between the A series and the B series.

Back to archaeology

So, how does all this help archaeology? Perhaps it is helpful to put these philosophical debates into an archaeological context so their relevance is made explicit. The traditional archaeological conception of time as expressed through chronology or evolutionism can be seen as the B series view of time: time as a succession of points (i.e. periods, years, stages). Childe made this explicit many years ago: 'Archaeological time exhibits seriation but not duration' (Childe 1956: 58). Yet, clearly, as the philosophical debates reveal, time is also duration, a flux which has tense and which the B series cannot represent. One could argue that the B series is enough, that it even corresponds to an objective or scientific view of time, while the A series is purely subjective and has no role in archaeology. But as the philosophical arguments show, this is misleading, since a B series without an A series is hardly time at all – indeed, it is simply succession and, moreover, one unable to deal with the question of change. This is very clear in the case of traditional evolutionism, which rests upon the B series – it cannot really explain change at all, as change is ultimately subsumed to a succession of stages.

But now let us consider the approaches taken by archaeologists influenced by the *Annales* school or non-linear dynamics. For them, the core of the problem revolved around the dualism of continuity and change, process and event. They realized, implicitly or explicitly, that time is not simply a succession of moments but a duality of the line and the point, of duration and succession: the A series and the B series. By problematizing both continuity and change, they embraced a much fuller conception of time than represented in chronology or evolutionism. Like Husserl, they use the B series to represent time, but by using more than one scale of time, they are able to create a temporality that has depth, that has more than one dimension and, therefore, is able to express the duality. Of course, the same criticisms of Husserl apply to these approaches, in that, ultimately, they still depend on the B series to represent time even if they are multiplied through different scales. But then, perhaps this just recognizes the fact that time is, in essence, paradoxical and all we can do is try to approximate it.

By using different scales in archaeological analysis, just as Husserl used two dimensions of succession and retention to represent the multi-dimensionality of temporal experience through the oblique line, a much richer representation of time is created. One of the problems with the B series view of time is that it represents time through a spatial metaphor; perhaps this is unavoidable, but by using multiple dimensions, something of the non-spatial nature of time can be captured in an analytical manner. Indeed, it is often said that time is just one dimensional while space has three; but, under this new conception of time, it too can be said to have three or more dimensions. Time is conventionally represented as a point/line, but by adding another point/line at right angles as Husserl did to express the flux of time, time has also, in effect, acquired multiple dimensions. However, Husserl's diagram was only abstract; we can actually modify Husserl's diagram to make it better represent the non-linear models of historical change described above. We can do this by suggesting that perhaps different events have different 'echo' or retention lengths, which might correspond to the different temporal scales used in *Annales* or non-linear dynamics explanations of change. Thus, at any point in time, the 'echo' or resonance of past events will have variously different effects or impact on the present according to the length of their 'echo', and something from further back in time might actually have more impact on something more recently past because of this (Figure 1.6). Thus, in the example, if the present is G, then only previous events B, D and F have a trace in G (solid lines), but not A, C or E (dashed lines). This 'weighting' of

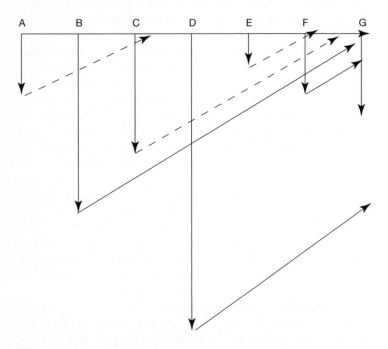

Figure 1.6 Husserl's diagram applied to non-linear models of archaeological change.

events with differential duration enables us to see the basic similarity of Husserl's description of time with non-linear models of change.

It is now time to leave behind these ideas and bring this chapter to a conclusion. I started by looking at the conventional way archaeology perceives time, specifically discussing the notion of chronology. I then suggested that chronology presented a very particular view of time, as a linear sequence, and suggested that this has greatly influenced traditional interpretations of cultural change. Cultural evolution, as articulated in terms of a social typology and stages of historical change reproduces the same basic temporal structure as chronology. By looking at more recent attempts to re-think the nature of change in the past, especially approaches influenced by the French historical school of *Annales* and also by theoretical developments of non-linear dynamics in natural science, an alternative conception of time was brought out. This view encapsulates more fully the philosophical complexity of time as expressed in terms of a duality or tension between two types of time – as a sensual flux and as abstract succession.

This first chapter is entitled 'Beyond chronology' and that is exactly what I have tried to do here – to go beyond chronology and see how re-thinking the concept of time can open up new possibilities of doing archaeology and interpreting the past. Indeed, that phrase can work as a suitable subtitle to the other chapters, and to this book as a whole. However, this must not be taken as a call to abandon chronology – it remains a vital and essential part of archaeology. I do not see how archaeology could function without it. Rather, it is an attempt to start thinking about additional ways in which other perceptions of time can enrich the discipline. So far, most of this discussion has been focused on looking at the relation between chronology and explanations of cultural change, and drawing out, usually implicit, meanings and perceptions of time in these explanations. In ending, I would like to move on and present the way other archaeologists have started to examine the concept of time and how this impacts the discipline. Here, discussion will move away from issues of social change and broaden out to cover a whole range of other problems, some of which may reference the philosophical issues already raised, while others will expand and develop them.

Theorizing time in archaeology

Discussion of the concept of time in archaeology has been virtually non-existent until recently. Earlier archaeologists who discussed the concept, tended to do so in relation to other issues, specifically the construction of chronologies. However, an interesting departure from this was a paper published in 1951 by Arden-Close who wrote about time in relation to memory, in particular about the recovery of the thoughts of people in the past through written testimonies, oral histories, myths and legends, and even fiction (Arden-Close 1951). However, papers like this hardly constitute a discourse on time. Proper examination of the concept of time in relation to archaeological theory and method did not really begin until the late 1970s and 1980s. One of the first archaeologists to seriously examine the concept of time was Mark Leone in a paper called 'Time in American Archaeology' (Leone 1978). He argued that archaeologists rarely, if ever, looked at how past societies viewed time, or how our own conception of time affects our interpretations of the past. Drawing on the optimism of Binford and the New Archaeology, where *all* aspects of past societies are potentially open to archaeological investigation – not just technology or economy but also ideology – Leone suggests that archaeologists can see past perceptions of time in the archaeological record. In particular, Leone drew attention to the ideological status of time, both in how past societies viewed time and how archaeologists view it.

A much more detailed study a few years later was carried out by Geoff Bailey who, in two papers published in the early 1980s, expressed much the same sentiments as Leone regarding the lack of discussion on time (Bailey 1981, 1983). Bailey also distinguishes the same two issues as Leone, namely, past societies' perception of time and archaeologists' perception of time and, ultimately, argues for seeing them as connected (see below). However, Bailey does take quite a different angle on the question of time, focusing his discussion through the theory of time perspectivism. I will discuss this in much more detail later in the next chapter but, broadly, this theory argues that different processes or phenomena operate at quite different temporal scales (e.g. long term and short term) and, therefore, require different approaches. This is linked to the espousal of timescales by *Annales* theory and non-linear dynamics discussed above, but has more methodological implications that were not raised there. Bailey's own emphasis was on long-term processes as he thought these were especially, if not uniquely, an area for archaeological investigation.

Bailey's views were summarized in a shorter paper published in 1987 for a themed issue on time for the *Archaeological Review from Cambridge*. In the same volume was a completely different paper on time by two other Cambridge archaeologists, Michael Shanks and Christopher Tilley (Shanks and Tilley 1987a). They addressed the issue of time from a post-processual angle, an examination pursued in greater detail in their book *Social Theory and Archaeology*, also published in 1987. They critique Bailey's papers, but also go on to present a more radical view of time that is much closer to Leone's, where they reassert the ideological nature of time, in particular associating the archaeological concept of time – specifically chronology – with the modern capitalist worldview. They go much further than Leone in deconstructing this modern concept of time and, rather than distinguish objective and subjective time, they suggest a very different axis of difference: the abstract and the substantial. Abstract time is the modern capitalist perception of time; time consisting of measurable units and separated from events, from history. This is time as chronology. Substantial time, on the other hand, is a time more closely conceived in traditional societies, time that is embedded in events and history; marked rather than measured.

These early papers by Leone, Bailey, Shanks and Tilley all emphasized a lack of discussion on time in archaeology, and can be seen as consciousness-raising texts as much as anything. They were the first to put time on the agenda in theoretical archaeology. They were all written around the time post-processualism was emerging as a new theoretical paradigm (Hodder 1985), yet only Shanks and Tilley's texts could be fairly described as post-processual. It would be more accurate to say that this new discourse on time fell within a larger phase of theoretical development, which included post-processualism but, more generally, saw a reassessment of processual theory, some of which was radically anti-processual, while another part was more about developing processual theory in new directions. The studies discussed so far rarely developed the ideas much beyond critique – with, perhaps, the exception of Bailey. It was not until the 1990s that more substantive research started to appear.

Some of the earliest case studies that had implications for theorizing time, were those that more explicitly looked at history and social change than time itself, particularly those drawing on the *Annales* school or non-linear system modelling, as discussed above. However, in terms of more specific time theory, it is probably fair to say there have been two strands, more or less following the broad divisions identified by Leone and Bailey: studies on past societies' perceptions of time and reviews of archaeologists' perception of time. The early 1990s saw the emergence of new investigations into prehistoric perceptions of time, especially the way social memory is articulated in material culture. Two volumes of the journal *World Archaeology* have been devoted specifically to this issue (in 1993 and 1998), and since then there have been several publications devoted to this topic (e.g. Gosden 1994; Bradley 2002; van Dyke and Alcock 2003). Similarly, over the same decade there have been critiques and alternative presentations of how archaeologists conceive time in relation to both the archaeological record and the construction of archaeological narratives. Debates about the relations between the present and the past, origin stories (Conkey and Williams 1991; Moore 1995) and artefact biographies (Appadurai 1986; Thomas 1996; Holtorf 2002a) all express different temporal conceptions. More recently, there have been studies on how a critical examination of time can impact on our understanding of the archaeological record and material culture at its most basic level (Gosden 1994; Thomas 1996; Murray 1999b).

There is little doubt that discussion of time has been slowly increasing since Leone's paper in 1978, although it is only since the 1990s that this has built up anything like a critical momentum. Moreover, as this brief survey demonstrates, there is quite a diversity of approaches, some complementary, others more radically divergent. The different aspects of time in archaeology and the different theoretical inspirations will probably sustain this diversity, as the recent publication of the first two whole volumes dedicated to the subject demonstrate (Murray 1999a; Karlsson 2001a). Nevertheless, considering time is such a central concept in archaeology, it is surprising it has taken so long for this degree of discourse to develop – especially when one considers that papers and volumes on space first appeared in the 1970s (e.g. Clarke 1977; Hodder 1978; Hodder and Orton 1976). Why the discussion of time has lagged so far behind similar discourses on space is something I touch on later in the book. In the next two chapters, therefore, I want to explore in more detail the two strands of time theory identified, and show how a critical awareness and conception of time can change the way we do archaeology.

2

TIME AND THE
ARCHAEOLOGICAL RECORD

Time, space and the archaeological record

I would like to start by contrasting the nature of space and time as methodological issues in archaeology. It takes no serious reflection to discern a major disparity in archaeological control over space and time as they are traditionally understood, i.e. space and time as measures or dimensions of archaeological analysis. For archaeologists, space in this sense has never been problematic – we have always been able to measure the spatial parameters of, say, a site, using local or national grids, or, more recently, GPS. But time has not been so amenable. Despite the advent of radiocarbon dating since the 1950s, the temporal location of archaeological entities in an absolute framework (usually calendar years) remains fuzzy, and requires effort, expense and a suitable context that normally means that a single date, or a handful of dates, stand as proxies for a whole site or phase of a site – or even a whole artefact type. Moreover, excepting where historical dating can be used, our absolute dates may only be good to within half a century or so. Unlike spatial location, we cannot provide as tight a dating framework for anything we choose – both the degree of resolution of our methods and its applicability limit what we can do. This is not to be pessimistic about our dating techniques – the situation today is undoubtedly a staggering improvement on the situation half a century ago, and new techniques or refinements of old ones are constantly being made that only increase our ability to date our material. The point I would like to make is, rather, that dating is, and probably always will be, problematic compared to spatial location, because we do not have the same degree of control over its measurement.

But perhaps this asymmetry between space and time is only problematic under a certain conception of time – indeed, perhaps it is problematic *only* because time is largely defined in reference to space in the first place. For example, when we excavate a site, we recover house plans or artefact distributions, and when we conduct a field survey, we record settlement patterns and enclosures. The spatial attributes of the archaeological record, though of course modified – and I discuss this below – are there, part of what we uncover. What we do not dig up, though, are life cycles of objects or households, historical processes of change. For these temporal attributes, we are forced to infer from variation in the spatial ones using chronology as a control. But even most of our chronological methods are spatial in derivation – for example, in stratigraphy, above and below are translated into later and earlier, in typology or seriation, formal difference in design is translated into temporal difference or change. Thus, it would seem that spatial variation usually forms the basis for inferring temporal variation. But is this really an accurate representation of the archaeological record?

An important debate between two North American archaeologists, Michael Schiffer and Lewis Binford in the early 1980s, raised this question, though obliquely. Schiffer began the debate by exploring the theoretical issues surrounding the nature of the archaeological record and, particularly, promoting the importance of understanding site formation processes in interpreting the past. He made a distinction between the archaeological context (e.g. the archaeological site) and the systemic context (e.g. the past cultural system that created the site), and moreover, pointed out that the archaeological context is not a direct representation of this systemic context but has undergone various changes that result from processes he called *transforms* (Schiffer 1972, 1976). Binford attacked this representation because it implies that the archaeological record is *distorted* – and one can only suggest this if one views that record as originally a kind of 'Pompeii', that is, a frozen record of a living cultural system at one particular moment in the past (Binford 1981). Binford makes an important point but he does not seem to realize its full implications; for although he argues against the notion of distortion and thus the distinction between an original and a transformed archaeological record, he still agrees with Schiffer on the distinction between the archaeological and systemic contexts.

Crucially, Binford characterizes the archaeological context as *static*, in distinction to the *dynamic* nature of the systemic context. Although it may not be Pompeii, the archaeological record is still a fossil. Thus, Binford suggests that the archaeological record is in many ways a palimpsest, the cumulative remains of multiple past processes, and does not reflect any particular moment in the past as if frozen through a catastrophic event such as at Pompeii. But whether a frozen moment or a static accumulation of events, the record is still regarded as frozen or dead. Binford's critique was very much directed at the concept of *transforms* and not formation processes per se and Schiffer's later work largely reaffirms the distinction between systemic and archaeological context, and that moving from one to the other requires the study of formation processes (Schiffer 1987). This model remains the generally accepted view on the archaeological record, and is often represented by a diagram of how the systemic context undergoes various changes before it becomes the archaeological context (Figure 2.1). It is precisely this view that underscores the idea discussed above, that time and temporal phenomena are derivative of space.

But is this right? To some extent, it was recognized even by Schiffer that the archaeological record is dynamic, at least in the sense that it continues to be affected by post-depositional processes. Archaeological remains are always subject to attrition, for example, from natural processes such as erosion and bioturbation. But in so far as it relates to the past systemic context, the archaeological context is static. However, as the post-processual slant on the Binford–Schiffer debate makes clear, it is not just natural processes that are still affecting the archaeological record, it is also contemporary social processes, most particularly the

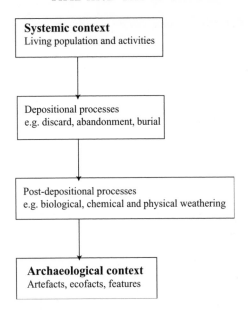

Figure 2.1 Model showing the transformation from systemic to archaeological context.

archaeologists themselves. The archaeological record is always dynamic, indeed, is always part of a systemic context, whether it is above or below ground. If it is visible and tangible, then human societies will always have to work out their relationship to it, even if this means choosing to ignore it. Indeed, this very recognition makes it possible to explore past people's perception of the past – a topic discussed in more detail in the next chapter. Stonehenge is not just a prehistoric monument – it is also a Roman one, a Medieval one and a contemporary one, no matter whether it has been physically intervened with or not (e.g. Thomas 1996: 62–3; Bender 1998).

This is not to deny that past remains do slip out of human history – chiefly by being buried – but even when they do, they remain part of the landscape and its natural processes (I discuss this further below). The archaeological record, therefore, is always dynamic, not static, and when archaeologists excavate a site, these remains continue to exist in time as well as space. The distinction between the archaeological and systemic context is, in fact, invalid and, more importantly perhaps, so is the separation between the past and the present (Thomas 1996: 55–64; also see Barrett 1988; Patrik 1985). By arguing for a static archaeological record, Binford and others by default also create an impenetrable barrier between the past and the present, and the only way this barrier is crossed, is through chronology – that is, a universal time that is independent of any events. As soon as one wants to bring events back into the picture, they will always remain divided into two types – past events and present events. In other words, this view of the archaeological record and the view of a universal, independent time, as expressed in chronology, are mutually reinforcing.

If, on the other hand, we were to argue that time is in fact situated, embedded in life and events, then we can no longer maintain the separation of past and present, or view the archaeological record as static. Drawing on the philosophy of phenomenology in relation to time, especially the work of the German philosopher Heidegger, several archaeologists have argued just this (Thomas 1996; Gosden 1994; Karlsson 2001b). This view of time is radically different from chronology, and suggests by implication that the distinction between the archaeological record and the archaeologist is not that sharply defined – nor indeed, is that between the archaeologist and past societies. This does not deny the past as a problem of interpretation, as Thomas makes clear – rather it denies any sharp break (Thomas 1996: 61). The past is, indeed, a problem of interpretation, and perhaps in no way more so than when it has been 'forgotten' (Lucas 1997). The very resurrection and irruption into the present of material remains from the past, after a period of burial, often presents a conceptual challenge to any society that 'discovers' them. Whether it is Roman farmers uncovering prehistoric remains in the course of ploughing their fields, or a modern day archaeologist on an excavation, the question of what these remains are and what they mean becomes an interpretive problem. But it is a problem only exacerbated if it is presumed from the start that somehow those remains have no temporal connection to the present.

Palimpsests and timescales

If we argue that the archaeological record does have a temporality then we are challenged to find new ways of thinking about that record. To that end, it is useful to salvage one idea of the old static notion of the archaeological record – and that is the notion of *palimpsest*. Given the textual metaphors used by many post-processual archaeologists for the archaeological record, the concept of palimpsest is rather apt (Patrik 1985). Originally meaning a manuscript on which earlier writing has been effaced to make way for new text, translated in terms of the archaeological record, it refers to the traces of multiple, overlapping activities over variable periods of time and the variable erasing of earlier traces. The concept of palimpsest is certainly very different from any 'Pompeii Premise', but its real value only emerges if we recognize that a palimpsest is not akin to layering, but a rather messier affair. Indeed, the true nature of the archaeological record comes out if we compare it to any scene around us in everyday life. Consider this by the French archaeologist Laurent Olivier, as he writes a paper on time in archaeology:

> The house where I am writing this paper was built towards the beginning of this century, in the courtyard of an ancient farm whose structure is still visible. From my open window, I see an interweaving of houses and constructions, most of them dating back to the 19th century, sometimes including parts of earlier constructions from the 18th or 17th century. The 20th century here looks so localized, so secondary: it is reduced to details, such as windows, doors or, within houses and flats, furniture . . . . Right now, the present here is made up of a series of past durations that makes the present multi-temporal.

(Olivier 2001)

Olivier has used this notion of a multi-temporal present to examine the past most effectively in his study of an Early Iron Age burial in Germany, the Hochdorf 'princely' grave (Olivier 1999). Here, he distinguishes three different 'periods' associated with the funerary assemblage of this burial: the period covered by the deceased's lifetime, the period between the death of the person buried and interment of his corpse and, finally, the brief period of the interment itself. Each of these periods is associated with different elements of the funerary assemblage – thus, certain items such as clothing and jewellery were considered to belong to the individual and thus have a temporality linked to his life cycle. Looking at signs of wear and repair usually indicates such objects. Other components, however, probably happened after the person died – such as the gilding of many of his personal possessions (shoes, dagger, drinking horn), while others such as food offerings (e.g. a honey and water mixture) belong to the final period of interment. Such multi-temporality obviously has implications for the dating of the grave, but more importantly, conceptually it shows how what appears to be even a single event in the past, can actually incorporate a palimpsest of multiple events and time-scales.

Such recognition of the multi-temporal nature of the archaeo-logical record suggests that even at its most basic level, archaeological frameworks for thinking about material culture need radical modification. To illustrate this, I will examine how sites and landscapes are conventionally characterized temporally and how this reproduces the sequential, chronological model of time, even when using apparently complex modelling such as the Harris Matrix (Harris 1989). I suggest that we need to add greater temporal complexity to this model by considering other aspects of time beyond sequence. To begin with sites; how do we understand the temporality of a site? The overriding method throughout the discipline's history has been through the use of phasing – that is, dividing up the features into different periods or phases. How this phasing is worked out in practice has changed, of course, although the basis has usually been on strati-graphic relations. Stratigraphy in the earlier part of this century was typically conceived very much in geological terms, in particular as the superposition of layers one upon the other. In a very simple situation, such as cave archaeology, this geological approach provided the perfect analogy with phasing or period divisions read off as one layer gave way to another. Of course, this approach does not work so well on other sites such as urban or urban-type contexts where uniform, widespread layers separating major phases of activity do not occur, although the same approach was applied with features grouped into phase divisions (e.g. Kenyon 1953: 130–1). Today, it is more common to employ a different approach based on the Harris Matrix, developed precisely out of urban situations where the layer-based approach was least applicable (Harris 1989). The major difference between using matrices and older correlation methods was that the stratigraphic sequence was independent of the phasing process – one constructs the matrix and then groups sections on the matrix into phase or period divisions. In the old method, features were tied or correlated around layers whose stratigraphic position simultaneously provided the basis for phasing a site. There is little doubt that the use of the matrix allows much greater flexibility and control in a complex stratified site, but there are problems.

Despite its appearance as a multi-linear model, ultimately the matrix is still a simple causal chain, a sequence of events one following the other; even allowing for multi-linearity, the temporality of the site is, essentially, the temporality of *sequence*. And in this respect, it is little different from periodization; indeed, the matrix might be seen as periodization writ small. The adjunct to this view is that the individual deposits or stratigraphic units, themselves, possess no temporality, they are just points in the series. A floor, for example, may have been laid *before* a hearth or oven was constructed on top of it, but the floor itself as an active, *used* surface, may endure as long as, if not longer than, the hearth. The matrix only shows the temporality of production, not use. And this has been a major criticism of the matrix – that it does not refer to how long a deposit took to form or how long a structure was in use (Lucas 2001: 161–2). This problem – that the temporality of sequence is divorced from that of duration – has been raised before, notably by Magnus Dalland but more force-fully by Martin Carver (Dalland 1984; Carver 1990; also see Harris' response, 1991).

The key issue here is the separation of duration from sequence in the temporality of a site; despite the sophistication of a model such as the matrix, it utilizes a very simple model of time – as sequence (the B series – see Chapter 1). Yet, as most archaeologists are aware, this reduces the temporal complexity of a site, and alongside the formalism of the matrix or phasing, we always have to retain a more informal recollection of this other temporality – duration. For example, when understanding the association of finds with a deposit, a key factor is recognizing how long the deposit took to form, *irrespective of its place in the sequence*. Was it deposited rapidly by human action or was it the product of slow natural silting? If rapidly, we may consider the finds more closely contemporary than if the deposit had accumulated slowly – it might even enable us to differentiate whether any age variability in a finds group was reflective of what was in use at any particular time, as opposed to what had simply accumulated on the site. However, the issue extends beyond the interpretation of finds assemblages to the nature of how a site temporality is represented. If we view the site solely as a sequence, it encourages us to see its components atemporally and in many ways, despite the multi-linearity afforded by the matrix, to still carve up the site into discrete phases. Consider a hypothetical Bronze Age landscape in southern England – it is composed of Early Bronze Age barrows, Middle Bronze Age field boundaries, and a Late Bronze Age settlement. Now, seen purely in terms of a sequence of production and phasing, we might produce a plan showing each element succeeding the other, as shown in Figure 2.2(a). Yet, if we recognize that the barrows and field system will still be extant in successive phases, then the phasing plans look very different (Figure 2.2(b)) and, more importantly, may help us to understand aspects of each phase in question. Thus, the arrangement of the field boundaries only makes sense because they reference the earlier barrows and, likewise, the settlement references the boundaries. This is a fairly obvious example, but it does illustrate something we may forget when dealing with more complex sites, in the compulsion to separate out a 'mess' of features. More critically, it highlights the importance of duration and temporal closure over features or stratigraphic units which conventional phasing and stratification elides.

The advantages to this second type of representation are that they both show duration and also allow the possibility of multiple phases simultaneously; for example, because different components of a site endure for differing lengths of time, there are different rates of change occurring on the site. Moreover, this can even be used to try to understand the experience of change and temporality at any given moment by the inhabitants of a site, as it will be dependent on what aspects of their space or material world are changing. A whole complex of temporalities is potentially identifiable and one may get a richer sense of how the passage of time may have been perceived through the way different elements change at different rates or scales. We can actually illustrate this by looking at two different ways of perceiving and representing the historic landscape around us today. Traditional approaches, associated with reconstructions of past landscapes, attempt to emphasize the appearance of landscapes during one particular period or phase of the past. Stonehenge, for example, is very much presented as a Bronze Age monument in a Bronze Age landscape; the fact that it was also a landscape in the Roman and later periods is largely elided. On this view, the present-day landscape as a whole is presented as a series of fragments of different periods, each surviving to varying degrees, usually according to their antiquity (Figure 2.3(a)). However, an alternative perspective, exemplified by the English Historic Landscape Characterisation project (Aldred 2002), suggests the present-day landscape is not so much a collection of fragmented, fossilized landscapes of different periods but, rather, a historical process incorporating multiple temporalities which have different resonances in the present day (Figure 2.3(b)). This multi-layered temporality is much richer than the fragmented image of fossil landscapes, and it enhances our appreciation of the inter-connectedness of the past and the present. Translating the same approach to *past* landscapes

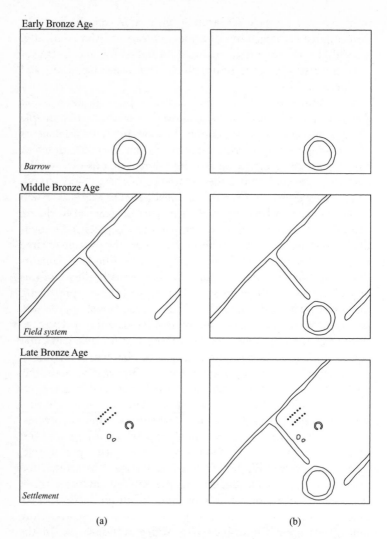

Figure 2.2 Alternative representations of a Bronze Age landscape over time.

and sites will actually help us to understand how people in the past experienced their past and time, a theme taken up in more detail in the next chapter.

This example reveals how the traditional view of time as chronological sequence is only a partial view of time, and one that seriously misrepresents the nature of the archaeological record. It affects the way archaeologists order and configure their data at a very basic level which can only be detrimental to higher levels of interpretation and synthesis. In suggesting alternatives, an approach that was more attentive to the multi-temporality of the archaeological record was used, to show how a different way of configuring the data is possible. The archaeological record is a palimpsest of multiple temporalities, and any simple reduction of this through the chronological sequence does it a serious injustice. Whether a single object, a single feature, or a whole site or land-scape, time is inscribed in its very constitution at multiple levels and scales, to such an extent that to ask a simple question like, 'what date is it?', is perhaps not just difficult because of our in-ability to control chronology, but because the very question presupposes too simplistic a view of time.

Time perspectivism

One of the most important recognitions to come from the previous section is that time is multi-layered; change and events happen at different scales or over varied periods of time and, more importantly, the very constitution of objects is determined by this temporality. The implications of this are crucial for archaeological interpretation, indeed, it suggests that time is not simply a con-tainer or something separate from objects but part of their very definition. If we accept this, then we need to consider the role time plays in the nature of archaeological explanations – in particular, how the chronological resolution afforded to archaeologists might affect such explanations. For example, some time ago it was suggested that the distinction between normative and behavioural explanations is largely a difference in degree rather than kind, according to a scaling of time and number of people

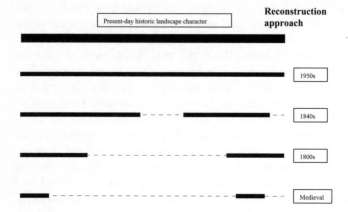

Reconstruction without necessarily indicating in what way different periods have contributed to the character of later period.

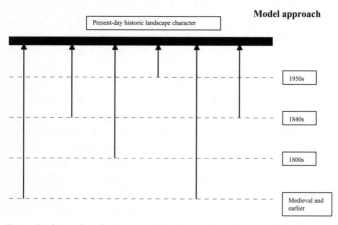

Connecting interactions that have contributed to the form of present-day landscape.

Figure 2.3 Alternative approaches to the contemporary landscape.

(Brooks 1982). Brooks suggested, alongside a threefold division of people from individual to community, a three-tier temporality for activities: events (single activities), episodes (groups of daily events) and series (groups of occupational episodes). He suggested that the more normative explanations were not simply associated with the generalized social group but also with a generalized timescale of the series. The implication is that chronological resolution will affect how specific one's interpretation can be.

Brook's paper, however, primarily focuses on a short-term temporality – he is clearly taking his cue from an ethnographic timescale rather than a historical one. Bailey was one of the first to suggest that in the context of the Pleistocene, and Palaeolithic archaeology generally, the timescales one typically deals with are vast and, thus, one should employ quite a different type of explanation from that used in historical archaeology, for example (Bailey 1981, 1983). Others, such as Fletcher (1992), have developed the arguments for time perspectivism further, but it is Murray who has discussed them in most detail (Murray 1993, 1997, 1999b). The key issue really hinges on this question of timescale: because the chronological resolution that prehistoric archaeology generally deals with, is quite long – in some cases millennia – then it really needs a unique method of explanation that cannot draw on any other social science discipline. History, anthropology and sociology do not work on the same timescales, so their theories cannot be adequately used in prehistoric archaeology. For Bailey, this actually suggests the strength and uniqueness of archaeology.

There have been criticisms of this, but I will defer them until later – certainly, many of the critiques of Bailey's papers are directed at a whole range of issues, not just his time perspectivism (Shanks and Tilley 1987; Squair 1994; see Murray 1999b for a rebuttal of these critiques). For the moment, I want to focus on the implications of time perspectivism and, particularly, on the idea that social theory derived from ethnographic timescales is not *enough*, nor always even suitable, in understanding archaeological data. Murray draws on the debates of the 'Pompeii Premise' and, especially, Binford to develop this argument. For Binford, archaeology is not about reconstructing 'prehistoric ethnographies' – the cultural or systemic context to which the archaeological record refers is not the same as the ethnographic context but something uniquely different (Binford 1981: 197–8). In short, archaeological and ethnographic cultures are not the same thing – archaeological cultures are more like dynamic systems that operate at different timescales. Although Murray does not necessarily agree with all of Binford's views, he does suggest that this basic recognition by Binford on the nature of the archaeological record needs to be taken seriously (Murray 1999b).

Ultimately, for Murray, as for Bailey before him, it is the unique timescales involved in the archaeological record, that make it different from data in other social sciences, especially ethnography. Consequently, an archaeology that draws its theory from disciplines such as ethnography to explain the archaeological record is not being sufficiently reflexive about the nature of this record. Indeed, as Murray argued in one of his earliest papers, it is precisely this reliance on ethnographic descriptions of prehistory since the nineteenth century that made us forget the significance of the discovery of the antiquity of humankind so quickly (Murray 1993). Moreover, if archaeology did pay more attention to building its own theories which better reflected the nature of its own data, then it might also be able to contribute something new to social theory and, thus, might also have an impact on other disciplines.

The question of timescales is certainly important when it comes to interpreting the archaeological record – and perhaps nowhere more so than in the context of the Pleistocene. However, it is misleading to suggest that the archaeological record, by its very nature, works on a different timescale to the ethnographic record. Laurent Olivier's reflections on the 'contemporary' farmhouse he writes in and the Hochdorf grave he studies, show quite perfectly how an archaeological context and a living 'ethnographic' context can treated in a comparable manner. This is not to deny the important differences, particularly the role of postdepositional formation processes, but as Murray points out in his discussion of Binford and Schiffer's position, such processes only confirm the ultimate similarity between the two. While Schiffer regards the systemic context as ultimately comparable to the ethnographic one, Binford does not. Yet, I wonder if there is not some misrepresentation of the nature of the ethnographic context here by Binford. As Olivier's example of the farmhouse shows, any observation of a living context contains multiple time-scales, indeed, a walk through any landscape will encompass vast stretches of time, even beyond the Pleistocene. The problem is, Binford characterizes the ethnographic context as something existing in one-dimensional time, the present, and contrasts this with the deep timescales of the archaeological record. But this characterization of the ethnographic present is simply *wrong*. Surely, the ethnographic context is equally enveloped in deep timescales and if that is the case, then this seriously blurs the distinction between ethnographic and archaeological contexts.

I think there is some conflation of issues here with regard to time perspectivism. One concerns the timescales that archaeological data span, the other concerns the level of chronological resolution available. Certainly, prehistoric archaeology deals with durations that far exceed any other discipline of human culture – and certainly if it seeks to explain those durations *through long-term patterns or structures*, then it is quite reasonable to argue for novel interpretations that are not available in traditional social theory (i.e. derivative of history or ethnography). And if this is all Binford is saying then fine – though it seems as if he is conflating an explanatory approach with inherent properties of the archaeological record. However, even granting the explanatory approach – in the first place, archaeology does not *have to* take the duration or timescale over which prehistory occurs as the unit of its analysis. Just because archaeology deals with tens of millennia does not mean it has to interpret prehistory through models that use comparably large timescales as their units of analysis. But what if that is all that is available – what if the chronological resolution is only good to the nearest millennium? This raises the next issue, and here I think another conflation has taken place – between 'real' time and chronological time. It is possible that we might not be able to track changes in the upper Palaeolithic record to the same degree of resolution as the Neolithic, or the latter to the same degree as historical archaeologies. But this is only a problem in chronological time – not in real time. Consider the following examples.

A later Neolithic burial may only be able to be dated to within a century using C14 – say some time between 2150 and 2050 BC. In contrast, a Roman burial, associated with coins, pottery and jewellery is dated to within two decades, c. AD 330–350. While this resolution will surely constrain narratives about burial practice in the Neolithic and Roman periods, it need not dictate the timescales – it is quite possible that in real time, the burial events that produced the archaeological records of the Neolithic and Roman burials respectively were of similar duration, and that the scale of the events that produced the archaeological record in both cases, is no different from any we might witness today. We could write a narrative of both burials that uses the same timescale, even though their chronological resolution is different. Comparing Neolithic and Roman burials is one thing, however, but what about the archaeological record of the Palaeolithic – especially the lower period? Here, timescales are not just centuries but millennia and, more importantly, the very nature of sites is often radically different. Well, even here, the archaeological record can reflect events in real time, such as the horse butchery site at Boxgrove, southern England, dating to around half a million years BP (Pitts and Roberts 1998). But even if one is dealing with just objects, they contain reference to very short timescales – a handaxe may only be dateable to the Acheulian, but its production may have only taken minutes. The study of the production of a Palaeolithic handaxe encompasses no different a timescale to the study of the production of an eighteenth-century gunflint. Just because we can date the gunflint to AD 1725 but the handaxe to only c.250,000 to 200,000 BP does not necessarily count for anything in this context.

Ultimately, I think the key point is that the archaeological record encompasses a multi-temporality – just as the living, 'ethnographic' context does. Certainly, archaeology, because it studies much longer time periods than any other humanist discipline, should consider theories and explanations that might *uniquely* apply to such a large time span. But there is nothing intrinsic to the archaeological record that determines this has to be so. Small-scale events are just as visible in the archaeological record as long-term patterns (see Shennan 1993); the only constraint comes through chronological resolution and how we respond to that in constructing narratives. A narrative that is closely dependent on chronology will be more severely limited by this constraint than other narratives. Recognizing this distinction between chronological time and real time – or, perhaps better, narrative time, is crucial. Indeed, I would suggest that this is exactly where time perspectivism falls short – its only under-standing of time is as chronology (as many of its critics have pointed out; e.g. Shanks and Tilley 1987; Squair 1994) and, there-fore, its conception of explanation is tied exclusively to this notion of time. In the next section, I want to consider the concept of narrative time more fully, and how this concept has been devel-oped in archaeology. It is certainly not argued that narrative time should replace chronological time, or can even be totally independent of it – but it does have the potential to liberate interpretations of the past from the constraints of chronology to a greater or lesser extent.

Narrative time

The nature of archaeological narratives has been discussed else-where (see Pluciennik 1999 for a review), my specific concern here is with their temporal structure and, equally, the view of time portrayed in their structure – regardless of the specific content of the narrative. In a recent book, Joyce has touched on the theme of time and narrative structure in archaeology, and she uses the concept of chronotope after Bakhtin, to examine how particular genres of archaeological writing portray space and time (Joyce 2002: 34–8). She suggests there are two main chronotopes in archaeology, one of progress and one of discovery; in the former, time is portrayed as linear and directional, while in the latter, simply as 'now' or the moment. By implication, these two chronotopes can be linked with the temporal voice or tense of the narration – later in the book, Joyce contrasts a narrative that is retrospective ('it happened in the past') to one that is more predictive and closer to a running commentary of events as they unfold ('as it happens'; Joyce 2002: 54–5). Joyce is concerned with a whole range of other issues in her book, so does not go into this topic in any depth; in this section, however, I want to examine in more detail this structure of narrative time and, in particular, focus on the chronotope of progress and voice of retrospect, as I think this is the dominant model in formal academic discourse today.

Perhaps the most common structure of narrative time comes through archaeological periodization, where prehistory is divided into a series of 'chapters' that unfold a narrative. The Three Age periodization of European prehistory, for example, is not simply a relative chronology but also a narrative chronology – or at least, it *was*. The progression of technology from stone to iron fitted quite well into contemporary nineteenth-century narratives of industrial progress; indeed, the affinity between the two may be much closer than we might think. In 1866 at the Museum of National Antiquities in Stockholm, Sweden, an exhibition of antiquities using Thomsen's Three Age System was quite explicitly modelled on an exhibition of modern, mass-produced industrial goods that was showing the same year (Almgren 1995). Involved in the exhibition were three of the most important figures in late nineteenth- and early twentieth-century Swedish archaeology – the Hildebrands (father and son) and Montelius. The narrative of technological progress in the Three Age System was something that slowly receded as the twentieth century progressed however, so much so, in fact, that in the 1930s, Childe felt obliged to revivify the narrative content of the system through a functional-economic interpretation (Childe 1935). Today, this periodization more or less remains empty of its original narrative content and is largely a relative chronology, devoid of any specific meaning. This is most evident in the fact that many interpretations of prehistory now cover time periods that cut across these old periodizations; whereas a nineteenth-century book on prehistory might divide its chapters strictly by period (e.g. Neolithic, Bronze Age, Iron Age), a modern one will re-assemble its divisions, even if it still uses the same nomenclature (e.g. Later Neolithic/Early Bronze Age, Later Bronze Age/Early Iron Age).

However, even if the old Three Age periodization no longer has a specific interpretive content, there are more subtle traces of its thinking that we still employ – indeed, these are probably more deeply sedimented ideas about narrative time that we usually take for granted. The first concerns simply the directionality of the narrative; the Three Age System was closely linked, as I have mentioned, with the idea of progress and, more broadly, an evolutionary narrative. This comes out most clearly in our everyday archaeological language such as the use of the terms 'upper' and 'lower' – whether to designate period subdivisions (such as the Palaeolithic) or a generic sequence on site. Upper is later, lower is earlier; there is a clear vertical scale of time implicit in this language that derives ultimately from narratives of progress. In case this might seem a little too tenuous a link – especially in the case of a sequence on a site where 'upper' must be stratigraphically later for example, it is instructive to look at East Asian archaeological terminology as used in Japan, Korea and China. Here, the terms are reversed – upper means earlier, and lower means later. Needless to say, East Asian stratigraphy is not inverted – but their pre-archaeological, historical narrative structures *are* (Barnes 1990). Even though Japan, for example, adopted European models of periodization and the notion of prehistory – in spite of a traditional model that did not recognize the very concept – nevertheless, it retains traces of this older narrative structure in its archaeological terminology (Figure 2.4).

As well as narrative directionality, there is also the question of narrative subdivision. Consider the Three Age System again for a moment – why *three* ages? It might seem that this is simply dictated by the evidence – stone, bronze and iron. But why not just two – stone and metal? Part of the reason lies in the historicity of the concept of a three age system, which partly goes back to the Renaissance revival of the Roman philosopher Lucretius, but was given its modern form in the eighteenth century by several French

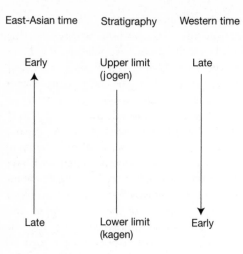

Figure 2.4 Japanese model of prehistory.

Source: Adapted from Barnes 1990.

antiquarians including, most famously, Goguet whose work was translated into English (Trigger 1989: 60). Additionally, Childe suggested that it was inherent in the very process of constructing chronologies through a process he called *tripartition*; although he does not explain it very clearly, the idea is that to place any two assemblages or sites in chronological order requires at least three components – one exclusive to each assemblage and a third which they share in common (Childe 1956: 66). However, more generally, three seems to be a golden number in narrative time – most of the prehistoric periods were also frequently divided up into three sub-divisions (early, middle and late, or A, B and C). What is the relationship here between such temporal divisions and narrative structure? The answer would seem to relate to classic genres of Western narrative and the association between history and cycles; as Collingwood suggested in 1927:

> a 'period' of history is an arbitrary fabrication, a mere part torn from its context, given a fictitious unity, and set in

fictitious isolation, yet by being so treated, it acquires a
beginning, and a middle and an end.

(Collingwood 1927: 324)

The point about historical narrative, according to Collingwood, is
its close connection to the idea of a historical cycle; the historian's
period is the structure behind the narrative – it provides the
parameters of the story and, like any story, will have a beginning,
middle and end: Early Bronze Age, Middle Bronze Age, Late
Bronze Age. But what Collingwood also recognized was the relativity of these periods – they are not real reflections of actual
cycles in history but constructions of the historian and can change
according to the point of view. Thus, the Early Bronze Age, once
the start of a narrative, is now so often the end.

However, in a couple of papers on material culture sequences,
Hodder has suggested that such cycles may, in fact, reflect something about the nature of the historical consciousness of past
people – and not just the archaeologist (Hodder 1993, 1995).
Hodder's suggestion comes from his application of hermeneutic
theory in relation to historical interpretation to the archaeological
record, and basically suggests that there is some connection
between 'archaeological' and 'past' narratives. In his discussion of
the sequence of the Greek tell of Sitagroi, he suggests that the
phasing had a real meaning for the people in the past – but rather
than rely on the heavily value-laden terms of linear progress or
cycles of rise and fall, he draws on modern narrative theory and
rhetorical tropes such as metaphor, synecdoche and irony. More
widely, he has applied the same model to his broader narrative of
the *domus* for Neolithic Europe, and uses tropes for characterizing
the shift from *domus* to *agrios* in the south Scandinavian Neolithic
(Hodder 1995).

It would be tempting to suggest all these examples somehow
capture a fundamental classification of narrative time, as linear
and cyclical. Even Hodder's aversion to drawing on these old
narratives of progress or cycle, does not altogether enable him to
avoid them (despite his recognition of this problem), as the adoption of these tropes often seems to mimic the same dual structure

of linear/cyclical. In the light of my misgivings of such a classification (see Chapter 3), I prefer to shift the discussion onto the
broader question of time and narrative, for the main value of
discussing these examples lies in revealing how time is implicated
in the very structure of narratives, especially through periodization and how this is used. Moreover, similar temporal structures
recur in other archaeological narratives, whether they are tied
to periods or not and, in conclusion, I will examine two: origin
stories and biographies.

Many archaeological narratives, past and present, produce
origin stories – the origins of agriculture, the origins of humans,
the origins of civilization. These projects attempt two things – to
define the essence of whatever it is (e.g. agriculture or civilization
or even humanity) and then fix the emergence of this essence in
chronological time. Conkey and Williams observed some time ago
that many archaeological narratives are such 'originary narratives'
(Conkey and Williams 1991). By this, they meant not only that
archaeologists have often been concerned with 'origins research' –
such as the origins of agriculture or the origins of the state but,
more fundamentally, they are concerned with 'originary meanings' – such as what this site or this artefact originally meant, as
if its *original* meaning is somehow its most *authentic* meaning.
Moore summed up this duality quite well:

> On the one hand, we look to the past for the origins of
> specific things, such as the state or sociality, language or
> gender, the family or sexual division of labour. On the
> other, we use the notion of origins to make a number of
> originary moves in our thinking and writing. These ori-
> ginary moves are designed to authorize certain accounts,
> to establish them as authoritative. These two aspects of
> the functioning of origins in the interpretation of the past
> work so as to produce continuous narratives.
>
> (Moore 1995: 51)

It is these 'originary moves' that are the key aspect here –
to seek the origins of anything presupposes to some extent, an

essentialist or originary meaning for that phenomenon. The problem has always been that defining the phenomenon in essentialist terms seems an ever-losing battle. What is agriculture? Is it cultivation or herding, or is it exploitation of domesticates? What of a society that cultivates wild wheat, or one that raids domestic livestock of neighbouring pastoralists? The problem is, we have a particular notion of what agriculture is today, and we back-project our understanding of this concept in contexts where it might simply not apply. Contemporary studies on the origins of agriculture tend to stress the aspect of transition rather than origin – i.e. transition from hunting and gathering to farming, because of this difficulty (Harris 1996: 1–2). However, it is still an originary narrative, because it is taking a modern concept and projecting it into the past. As Moore succinctly puts it: 'Our stories of the past must end with the present' (Moore 1995: 51).

Thus, in this sense, origins research reproduces a similar linear time as chronology, where the story of the past always ends in the present. The flipside of such originary thinking is what is known as 'the privilege of retrospect' (Squair 1994). Namely, that because we inhabit 'the future of the past', we have a special status in understanding the past that comes with hindsight. We can view events and patterns that were simply invisible to people in the past because they did not have the temporal distance we enjoy. This is part of Binford's argument about the distinction between the archaeological and ethnographic records discussed above – that because archaeologists can survey the past not only from a distance but at timescales beyond human life spans, they have a special privilege inaccessible to other social sciences (Binford 1986). Squair has criticized this privilege and what he calls the 'historical voyeur', most forcefully by invoking its presumption of closure; because the past *is* past, it is assumed to be closed and therefore determined and this is what endows the archaeologist with a special privilege (Squair 1994: 99–102). As Squair points out, however, just because the past is past, does not mean it is closed – this ignores the role of the present in constructing the past, it ignores the fact that *the past is only past, by virtue of its relation to the present*. This relation is obscured by a semantic sleight of hand where the present is characterized as the future of the past – in other words, the experiential terms of present, past and future are all interchangeable with the sequential terms of before and after – i.e. translated into chronological time (the 'B series'). But as we saw in Chapter 1, this relation of present to past cannot be characterized in this way without limiting the concept of time – the A series is not reducible to the B series. The past is not closed but open to the present, and retrospect is as much a burden as a privilege.

In many ways, Squair's critique misreads part of Binford's argument, especially about the issue of timescales (also see Murray 1999b), though I think the two issues – retrospect and timescales – need to be separated. Nevertheless, his critique of retrospect offering privileged insights because it is retrospective is valid, raising as it does the partiality of the temporal representation in its argument. Just as originary narratives ultimately assume an unproblematic link between the present and the past, so do arguments for the privilege of retrospect, for both pull the same trick of levelling time to the flat chronology of the B series in order to achieve this. To move towards an archaeology that does not make such presumption, in fact to one that actually embraces the multiplicity of time and does not level the A series to the B series, I want to explore a relatively new genre of archaeological narratives – biographies.

The idea of looking at biographies in archaeology – such as the biographies of objects – derives from a seminal volume of anthropological studies *The Social Life of Things* (Appadurai 1986). This concept is not simply the idea that objects have life cycles – this has been part of archaeological thinking since the 1950s or 1960s and is a key part of, for example, Schiffer's study of formation processes (Schiffer 1987: 13–15). More specifically, it is the notion that objects have a cultural history, that their meanings change through time and that the very historicity itself also imparts a meaning. In the context of originary thinking, for example, it quite clearly challenges any notion of an authentic meaning for objects or sites – each generation interprets the material culture around it in its own terms, whether that material culture is new or has been around for a long time. A Neolithic stone axe, for example, meant one thing to Neolithic people, but quite another to the Romano-British farmer who found it while preparing his field, or the eighteenth-century antiquarian who puts it in a glass case in his study. The meaning of the axe in Neolithic times (even assuming that it had one meaning then – which it almost certainly did not) is no more authentic or significant than that in later times – to privilege an originary meaning like this is to constrain our interpretation of the past. Neolithic axes that occur in Roman contexts or Saxon or Medieval contexts tell us something more about the object and history in general than if we simply confine ourselves to its Neolithic 'meaning'.

There have been various studies that look at biographies in this way (e.g. Thomas 1996: ch. 6), but I will discuss one of the most developed and sustained treatments as given by Holtorf in a series of papers (e.g. Holtorf 1998, 2002a, 2002b). Holtorf starts from the recognition of the multi-temporality of the archaeological record, that it is always a mixture of multiple times and that at any one time, past, present and future intertwine. As he says:

> We simply cannot isolate and study any period 'by itself': it is always also *its own past* as well as *our past*. People's thoughts and actions in the past were motivated by *their own future*, just like our own thoughts and actions (i.e. regarding past remains and people) are motivated by *our future*. Past, present and future are thus constantly intermingled with each other.
>
> (Holtorf 2002b: 187; emphasis in original)

Holtorf's multi-temporality raises questions over that explored by Olivier and discussed earlier; in Olivier's meditation on the farmhouse, for example, he remarks that the '20th century here looks so localized, so secondary' (Olivier 2001); yet, surely, everything around him was twentieth-century (at the time of writing), even the '17th century' remains that were re-interpreted and experienced in his present, the twentieth century. There is a hidden paradox in Olivier's reflections, in that his multi-temporality of the farmhouse is predicated on removing himself and his temporality from the scene. His perception, his position, is only possible if he pulls himself out of time, so he can compare seventeenth- and twentieth-century components; time, in Olivier's model, even if multi-temporal, remains chronological – it is just multi-chronological, if you like. Holtorf's point is that you cannot disassociate multi-temporality from temporal perspective.

In exploring this multi-temporality, Holtorf has taken prehistoric monuments as a key subject. In one of his earlier papers, he looks at a whole class of prehistoric monuments (megaliths) in Germany and examines their changing meaning over time (Holtorf 1996, 1998). However, in later papers, he challenges this earlier approach for its presumption of a stability of identity over time – in this case megaliths – as a stable subject of a biography. If a biographical approach is meant to show how meanings change over time, on what basis, then, does one preserve any object as the subject of a biography? What meaning does it have to trace a history like this if the only continuity is one imposed by the archaeologist – and one that, let's face it, ultimately could be accused of repeating an originary narrative? In response, Holtorf changes tactic and studies a single site or object rather than a class or type of monument. In two recent papers, he looks at the biography of an individual pot sherd and a single site in Spain (Holtorf 2002a, 2002b). His study of the site is more relevant to the discussion here because it fragments and re-orients many of the traditional goals of archaeological fieldwork; as he states, his methodology was guided by three principles: first, the site is not one site but, in fact, many sites; second, every material trace on the site is of equal significance, even yesterday's coke can; third, the aim of the investigation is not defined by a specific research problem but simply by the presence of the site itself.

The ultimate product of such a project is to collapse the conventional view of time as linear chronology and solely explore the site in terms of different pasts, presents and futures. The result is what Holtorf calls a 'non-linear chronology' for the site where different elements from different chronological periods are re-assembled from the straitjacket of a linear sequence into a network of

associations (Figure 2.5: also see Holtorf 1996 for a different interpretation of chronology and its distinction from chronography).
Holtorf's vision of this kind of archaeological narrative is quite
different from originary or other linear narratives as discussed
above. Indeed, it resembles the structure of hypertextual narratives that developed through web-based presentations, and which
have been argued as alternative ways of presenting archaeology
(e.g. Joyce 2002: 87–8; Hodder 1999). But such hypertext
presentations are often confined to the *representation* of the past
in non-linear ways – they do not necessarily challenge the narrative structure implicit in traditional practice (but see Shanks'
traumverk at http://.metamedia.stanford.edu/traumwerk/info.
html). Holtorf's vision is different in so far as it suggests the very
nature of fieldwork could be other than it is. For some, he may be
going too far but however one looks upon this kind of radical
narrative, it at least challenges us to reflect on the nature of our
narratives and the temporality they portray.

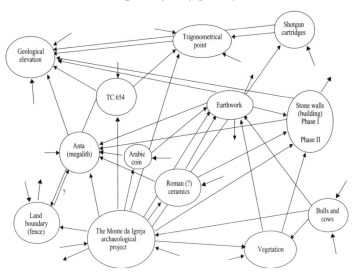

Figure 2.5 Holtorf's non-linear chronology.

Source: Courtesy of C. Holtrof, after Holtrof 2002a.

In many ways, the issue discussed above about narrative time is how conventional archaeological narrative tends to draw on the same conception of time as chronology: a directional, linear movement broken into divisions. In many narratives, these divisions follow periodization, but in most, some form of periodization is employed in structuring the narrative movement. Now, in so far as this structure is very similar to any narrative or story, with a beginning, middle and an end, I do not necessarily see this as a problem; there are other forms, such as the use of more fragmented texts or hypertexts and, while these are interesting alternatives, they do not seem to have the same appeal as the conventional story mode. Indeed, it has been argued that the conventional narrative mode is, in fact, an essential way of coming to terms with the paradoxes of time (Ricoeur 1988). But there are many other ways of addressing this issue – especially those that, perhaps, recapture the usually elided 'running commentary' narration that occurs informally during fieldwork. The chronotope of discovery is mostly marginalized in formal discourse but it has the merit of retaining the close connection between present and past, as well as presenting the processes through which archaeological knowledge is created. However, another way is to try to look at past temporalities, and actually make the concept of time part of the explicit subject of a narrative. In the next chapter, I will examine in more detail how archaeologists have explored a multi-temporal past by seeing how time was perceived in past societies and how this can be explored archaeologically.

3

TIME IN PAST SOCIETIES

Introduction: time in other societies

Time has always been an important concept in the social sciences as it pervades many different aspects of the study of human societies (see Adam 1990 for a review of the concept in sociology). More particularly, anthropologists have long been interested in how other societies perceive time (Munn 1992). Modern discussion of the subject in social theory can be traced back to Durkheim, who argued that the concept of time is embedded in social life and is, correspondingly, a social category of thought, re-working an original concept by the eighteenth-century German philosopher Kant (Durkheim 1915: 9–11). He noted, quite rightly, that it is impossible to talk about time except through the particular ways in which it is articulated in our society – such as our calendrical system and cycle of anniversaries and ceremonies. Phrases such as: 'last week', 'at four o'clock', 'at Christmas' and 'in 1997' are all very culturally specific. And even when we think we are familiar with something, there can be subtle differences that reveal alternate temporal perceptions. In English when I say 'half five', I mean half *past* five or 5.30; in Icelandic (*hálf fimm*) I mean half *of* five, or 4.30; failure to appreciate this subtle difference can cause major mis-understanding. This difference in an otherwise shared cultural time-consciousness not only can cause confusion, but expresses, albeit in a small way, a slight difference in the perception of time. In highlighting the importance of the social life of time, Durkheim opened the field, particularly for anthropological investigation of

61

how different societies conceive time. Many studies have been done on other societies' time perception, such as Bohannan's study of the Nigerian Tiv (Bohannan 1953), but among the earliest and most famous was Evans-Pritchard.

Evans-Pritchard provided the first, detailed ethnographic illustration of Durkheim's views based on his fieldwork among the Nuer of East Africa (Evans-Pritchard 1939, 1940). He showed how Nuer time-reckoning was linked to cycles such as the daily husbandry of cattle or seasonal activities, and also to generational cycles and the descent system. In particular, he argued in the case of genealogies, that for the Nuer, the temporal relationship or distance between the ancestors and any living person, *never* changes, even as one generation succeeds another. For us, this appears a completely illogical notion, but in the context of the Nuer lineage structure, it makes perfect sense. This perception of time is actually quite widespread ethnographically and might be more broadly characterized in terms of a distinction between mythic time or the time of the ancestors and present time or genealogical time. Lévi-Strauss characterized societies who held this view as 'cold' societies, in contrast to the 'hot' societies (such as European ones) that recognize history (Lévi-Strauss 1963, 1966).

One of Lévi-Strauss's main interests in terms of time was how 'cold' societies articulated the paradoxical relation between mythic time and present time. He suggested that various rituals served to overcome this paradox, particularly rituals that would seem to annul time by collapsing the distinction between the ancestral past and the living present (Lévi-Strauss 1966: 236). For Lévi-Strauss, 'cold' societies not only do not recognize history, but because they do not, they try to erase time and its effects altogether. Extending the distinction between mythic and present time into all aspects of time-reckoning, Edmund Leach claimed that non-Western or pre-modern societies regarded all time simply in terms of opposites – night and day, life and death, past and present (Leach 1961). This 'pendulum' theory of time is argued to derive from the primitive mind trying to conflate two temporal phenomena – repetition or natural cycles, and irreversibility or linear decay. Like Lévi-Strauss, Leach points to the role rituals play in articulating this 'pendulum' theory, especially their apparent ability to reverse time.

Since Lévi-Strauss and Leach, there has been a whole shift in anthropological thought, particularly away from broad generalizing distinctions between hot and cold societies. This distinction has been justly criticized, especially for the way it denies many societies a (sense of) history (Sahlins 1985; Wolf 1982), and anthropology has since been quick to explore this whole new field. Indeed, the interest in ethnohistories has been a growing field since the late 1980s with its emphasis on local genres of mythic-historical consciousness rather than a totalizing division of myth/history (Hill 1988). By focusing on the 'genre', the specificity of other cultures' attitudes to history can be disclosed. Harkin, for example, argues for the need to recognize the historical nature of human existence and, thus, the way indigenous people deal with this in their narratives (Harkin 1988); in particular, it is interesting how frequently narratives referring to the Contact period with European culture turn up (e.g. Harkin 1988; Hill 1988). Nevertheless, the original Durkheimian programme has not been abandoned, at least in terms of recognizing the cultural distinctiveness of different time perceptions. It has just become more sophisticated. Clifford Geertz's study of time-reckoning in relation to personhood in Bali is the classic example (Geertz 1973). He argues that in Balinese life, time is a 'motionless present' – by this he does not mean time is annulled or denied (as Lévi-Strauss might), but that the linear, cumulative flow of time is largely disregarded. He illustrates this through the Balinese calendar which, through a complex permutational system, does not so much mark time or the passage of time as mark the *kind* of time one is in at any particular moment.

Geertz's discussion has been criticized, most famously by Bloch who stresses a distinction between two areas of social life – the practical or everyday, and the ritual or ideological (Bloch 1977). Bloch argues that Geertz does not distinguish these two areas nor acknowledge that they entail quite different perceptions of time. He criticizes Geertz for solely discussing ritual time, and ignoring or downplaying the whole question of practical or everyday time-reckoning, which is more likely to encompass what we understand as linear time. Whether or not this is a fair critique of Geertz, in the process Bloch suggests that there are, ultimately, two kinds of time: universal linear time and relative cyclical time, the one associated with everyday practice, the other with ritual and ideology. This is, in many ways, an old distinction in social theory, that between linear and cyclical time, but Bloch gives it a new twist in tacit terms of a Marxist dichotomy of the organization of production (practical) and ideology (ritual) in hierarchical societies. However, it is not hard to find examples of cyclical time in everyday practice such as daily or seasonal work rhythms, which would seem to contradict Bloch's thesis. However, the key point Bloch is making is really to assert a universal time-consciousness and reject any strong argument for temporal, cultural relativism. By distinguishing practical from ritual time, Bloch is preserving anthropology from sliding into a cultural relativism which he sees Geertz as espousing (but see Geertz 1984).

And this really brings the discussion into the major debate in the anthropology of time – that is, to what extent is there a cross-cultural, universal time-consciousness? Or to put it another way: does recognizing cultural diversity in expressions of time-consciousness mean time is purely a cultural construct? Much of anthropological theory in the 1970s and 1980s was engaged in the whole question of cultural relativism, that is, to what extent do different societies share a basic universal rationality or is all thought completely culturally-determined (Hollis and Lukes 1982)? The issue about time is just one aspect of this more general question, and is often expressed as a dichotomy of objective and subjective time. The dilemma of cultural relativism is that on the one hand different societies do seem to think differently but, on the other, there must be some shared rationality otherwise there could be no communication or understanding between cultures. Anthropology therefore seems to be caught in a paradox – its *raison d'être* is to understand other cultures, yet, at the same time, show how different they are from us. The common way out of this dilemma has been to argue for a 'soft' and 'hard' version of cultural relativism, with anthropology usually taking the 'soft' option –

'soft' meaning cultures are different, but not *so* different. Where the dividing line of this difference occurs, is, of course, a question the soft option then feels obliged to engage with. For Bloch, this dividing line is effectively marked by the distinction between practical and ritual activity. But is it useful to separate social life into two areas as Bloch does, or is this not simply creating an artificial division to rescue anthropology from cultural relativism?

To a large extent, the debates about cultural relativism have moved on, and anthropology is rarely haunted by this phantom menace today. In the context of time-consciousness, though, it is worth being explicit about why this is not really an issue any longer. While it is fair to say that there may be a useful sense in which all societies or people share a common experience of time at some level, to talk about objective or universal time, distinct from subjective, culturally relative time creates more problems than it solves (see Munn 1992). At one level, to recognize *any* experience as temporal, subjective or objective is already to assert a common ground. But the notion that we could describe or articulate an objective meaning of time outside our own cultural frame is highly problematic. Moreover, it is important to recognize that what we think of as objective time is culturally specific to Western science and, especially, linked to the widespread use of clocks as scientific instruments (Tiles 1986). In this sense, scientific time is no more objective than any other time – it is equally embedded in the context of its use; in this case, science.

In practice, this means that scientific time is just one type of temporal perception among others, but with a privileged status in its own context, i.e. science. It would not help much to use Balinese time perceptions in studying planetary motion, and nor is scientific time much use in Balinese ritual. It might, however, be informative to use scientific time to study Balinese time; but this does not make scientific time more objective, it just makes it more commensurable. But then this is exactly what scientific time was developed for in the first place – this is its function, commensurability. Time as a measure. The important thing here is to recognize that time perception is linked to social life, to the context of its use, and science, like any other activity, is a part of modern social life (Latour 1999). To see scientific time in this way, robs it of none of its virtues, but removes the problems inherent in the objective–subjective dichotomy, as well as contextualizing scientific time.

In conclusion, none of this implies that all time is, therefore, subjective – the term subjective only has any meaning in opposition to objective and if we forgo the latter, we also forgo subjectivity as a concept. What there are, rather, are multiple times – both within any society and across societies, and while we may admit we can recognize different temporal perceptions as temporal, this does not necessarily mean we have to search for, or presume some fundamental, objective time. The issue here is ultimately one of communicability or intelligibility, not universality. A problem only arises when the explanation of intelligibility or the possibility of communication is placed primarily on an inherent, universal rationality rather than on the context of the communication. Anthropologists understand other cultures precisely because they live among the culture they study, because they interact with other people in living situations. Communication comes through the context of dialogue.

The most extensive and recent treatment of time in anthropology is undoubtedly Alfred Gell's dense monograph which ultimately presents a rapprochement between universal and relative time (Gell 1992). Gell draws heavily on the philosophical literature of time, particularly both the phenomenology of Husserl and the logical analysis of McTaggart, to create this rapprochement. Gell argues that there is no conflict in saying that time differs quite radically between different cultural contexts and, yet, maintaining that time remains a universal phenomenon experienced by all. Time-anthropology, for Gell, works best precisely when it recognizes this duality in a complementary rather than contradictory manner. He suggests, in fact, that studying another culture's time perception is best served by understanding them against more analytical studies of time such as cognition, time-geography and time-economics. Although Gell's sympathies leaned more towards the notion of an objective time than I have suggested here, I think the important point in all this it to recognize that accepting the cultural relativity of time-consciousness is *not* the same as accepting cultural incommensurability. Other societies do have different perceptions of time, indeed, the *same* society can have different perceptions of time, but that does not mean we cannot understand each other, or that we cannot talk about time in different ways in the same context. Time does not have to be a uniform or universal concept to be intelligible.

Time in past societies

The discussions about time in social theory clearly have implications for an archaeology that would want to explore the perception of time in the past. At the most fundamental level, the recognition of differences in time-consciousness among societies around the world suggests that prehistoric societies also had just as different temporal perceptions. The problem facing archaeologists, of course, is how to try to get at these perceptions. Attempts at this are fairly recent, largely because archaeology only started to address *any* conceptual or cognitive aspect of past societies after the 1960s, and it has only been since the late 1980s that this moved forward in any sustained manner. It was (and is) argued that how a society views the world is inextricably linked to their material relations with the world; that material culture encapsulates the conceptual, symbolic or cognitive structure of a society as much as its technology or economy. If this is the case, then temporal perceptions are equally implicit in the way past material culture is organized – it just needs looking for.

What does this mean in practice? Well, one approach could be to seek evidence of how time is marked in the past, i.e. evidence for time-reckoning. This might include anything from early clocks such as sun dials to alignments in structures which suggest astronomical observation. I will be discussing these approaches in this chapter, but if this was all that was meant by studying time in past societies, then archaeologists would be severely limited in what they could say. Indeed, not only archaeologists but anthropologists too. Around the same time as Durkheim published his influential work in which he discussed time, the Swedish ethnographer M.P. Nilsson wrote a book called *Primitive Time-Reckoning* (Nilsson 1920). In this work, he made an important distinction between two types of time perception: time-reckoning and time indication. Nilsson argued that all societies ultimately base their perception of time on two broad classes of natural phenomena: astronomical (i.e. the movements of the Sun, Moon and stars) and seasonal (i.e. climatic and biological cycles). However, only some societies have developed the observations of these natural phenomena into mathematical systems of time-reckoning such as the calendar; most societies simply indicate time by reference to these natural events (e.g. see Dietler and Herbich 1993; Turton and Ruggles 1978). Moreover, while time-reckoning systems employ regular divisions and continuous marking of time, time indication is irregular and discontinuous, what he calls *aoristic*. Nilsson presumed that time indication precedes time-reckoning, but as has been subsequently pointed out, time indication is just as much a feature of societies with time-reckoning systems as those without, indeed, often the two methods are in conflict (Pocock 1964).

Throughout this chapter, I will use the term time-reckoning in the very explicit sense outlined by Nilsson and in distinction to time indication; in other works, the term time-reckoning is taken in a more general sense of simply marking the passage of time (Munn 1992), but I think it is useful to retain Nilsson's distinction. Time indication, as opposed to systematic time-reckoning, is far more ubiquitous in all societies and, by implication, in the archaeological record. Most, if not all, archaeological sites should, at some level, contain some implications about time indication among the community who occupied that site. This will be evidenced through various practices that relate to the reproduction of the society, such as farming or ritual practices. Indeed, not only will certain activities be structured in a temporal manner (e.g. harvesting the crop at a certain time, burying the dead on a certain day), the temporal perceptions associated with the activity form an integral part of the nature of that activity. How easy it is to interpret such evidence is, of course, dependent on the nature of the material and the imagination and skill of the archaeologist, but the evidence is actually more abundant than we might think. The temporal structure of many activities in the past is something increasingly being recognized as central to an understanding of those activities. Two examples will suffice to demonstrate this.

The first is the fact that most environmental data has a seasonal aspect – plant and animal species exhibit life cycles that are often closely tied to specific parts of the year. At a Romano-British shrine in southern England, it was found that most of the sheep bones were juvenile and killed at a few months. This was used as an indicator that the rites performed at the shrine – or at least some of them – largely took place at one time of year, the spring (Legge *et al.* 2000). Once this association is made, this 'rite of spring' can be linked into other activities at the same time of year, but more importantly, it gives the ritual practice a much tighter definition and, perhaps, even suggests that other rites may also carry specific temporal associations. Does a spring rite have a different material signature to an autumn rite for example, and how might this manifest itself in other aspects of material culture, especially the deposition of artefacts? Not all sites might provide information to answer these questions, but they are worth exploring because they suggest that the temporal structure of ritual in Roman Britain may have been an important part of defining that ritual.

The second example concerns the temporal structure of production. In making anything from a house to a pot, there are usually a certain number of steps involved, a critical path through which production has to go for successful completion. There have been many studies in recent years that have looked at production in terms of behavioural or operational chains (Schiffer and Skibo 1997; Lemonnier 1993), and revealed the rich potential for understanding artefact design through the temporal structure of production. Of particular relevance here, though, van der Leeuw has pointed out the possibilities of exploring broader cultural conceptions of space and time through an examination of the operational sequence of an object (van der Leeuw 1993). He suggested that the same conceptualization surrounding the manufacture of an object such as a pot, may recur in other contexts since it reflects a deeper cultural perception of space and time. As an example, consider the construction of a house in the Neolithic of south-eastern Europe or Turkey; suppose that one of the last components to be built prior to occupation was the hearth or fireplace – this may be hard to demonstrate, but certainly as an internal feature it was probably built after the walls, floor and roof. How might the temporality of construction be evident in a wider context? If the building of the hearth was a final act of construction, marking the end of construction and the start of inhabitation, perhaps it gives greater resonance to the act of burning down houses so often observed in these regions (Tringham 1991). Perhaps the symbolic notion of the house as a hearth had temporal associations, in that just as the last act of construction involved the building of the hearth, so the last act of inhabitation involved literally turning the house into a hearth – i.e. setting it ablaze.

These two examples simply show that archaeology can explore time, in terms of the temporal structure of activities, in the past, and that this temporal *structure* will carry some implication for temporal *perception*. Society does not solely perceive time through time-marking systems, but through the very temporality of its practices and these offer the best avenue into the whole issue of time in past societies. Indeed, the two are so closely related that how time is marked or indicated is both determined by, *and* determinative of, the temporal structure of practice. As Munn remarks in the context of anthropology, it is probably better to talk about *temporalization* rather than time, i.e. time as a symbolic process (Munn 1992). In the rest of this chapter, I will explore two main types of approaches to time in archaeology. First, I will look at putative examples of possible time-reckoning systems in the past and argue that, in all cases, only time indication is unequivocally represented. There are real examples of time-reckoning systems in prehistory such as the calendrical systems of Mesoamerica or the dynastic lists of Old World cultures in China, Mesopotamia or Egypt. However, rather than discuss these examples, which are fairly unambiguous, I have decided to look at more troublesome cases in order to highlight the distinction between time-reckoning and time indication. The second approach is generally taken as the more useful one, and includes studies that look at the broader idea of time indication in relation to social practice. Here, the distinction between time-reckoning and time indication is less relevant, and what matters is the relation between marking the passage of time in general and the temporal nature of social practice.

Time-reckoning and time indication

One of the major areas of research into human perception of time in the past relates to hominid evolution and, specifically, the development of human cognition (Mithen 1992). A common strand of much of this research is the notion that human memory and the role of material culture as a mnemonic device plays a key part in mapping this evolution. In terms of Palaeolithic archaeology, discussion has particularly focused on a group of bone objects with serial marks cut into them which have been interpreted as systems of notation or tallies. This interpretation is fairly old and, in fact, goes back to the late nineteenth century, and although it has remained controversial, more detailed analytical work has taken this interpretation beyond mere speculation (Marshack 1972; d'Errico 1998). In particular, examining the method of marking (i.e. type of tool and its use) and changes in this method on the same object can support their interpretation as intentional tally or notation marks, even if the specific messages encoded are unknown. While d'Errico is more cautious of interpreting the meaning of such encoding, Marshack has been much more forthcoming, and suggests they relate to calendrical systems of notation (Figure 3.1).

Although these markings may indicate the use of mnemonic systems in the Upper Palaeolithic, their specific interpretation as time-marking must remain highly ambiguous. Nevertheless, as deliberate marking systems, they indicate that a new perception of temporality may have emerged at this time. These bone objects appear during the so-called 'big bang' of human consciousness or culture when archaeological evidence for a whole range of

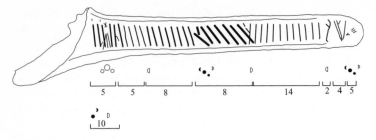

Figure 3.1 Markings on a Palaeolithic bone (*Placard bâton*) interpreted as a lunar calendrical system.

Source: Adapted from Marshack 1972.

new expressions emerge, such as art and religion – and possibly language (Mithen 1996: ch. 9). If the nature of human cognition did radically alter at this time, then it is quite likely that so did temporal perception. The fact that even early hominids could make stone tools (especially handaxes) shows foresight and the ability to plan ahead; clearly they had the ability to create temporal maps of some degree in their head. What these Upper Palaeolithic bone objects signify is the new development of an *external* temporal map, or an *artificial memory system* (AMS) as d'Errico has called them (d'Errico 1998). They allowed humans to extend the range of their memory and, perhaps more generally, the complexity of temporal mapping. Even if these bone objects do not relate to a time-reckoning system, they do suggest that for the first time in human evolution, it was possible in principle. It implies, at the least, the ability of time indication.

A similar approach has recently been taken towards some carved slate plaques of the later prehistory in Portugal and Spain, where the repetitive design motifs are interpreted as relating to lineage tallies – with clear implications for temporal reckoning by genealogy (Lillios 2003). In the context of mortuary rituals and ancestral cults, this seems a viable interpretation, if not equally difficult to support as Marshack's work. However, Lillios does make an important point about the lack of interest in such ideas, relating it to the implicit assumptions archaeologists make about prehistory as a time before writing. Because there are no written texts, we often presume that any notational system is either absent or beyond our grasp. The classic example of later prehistoric time-reckoning systems in Europe is, perhaps, equally ambiguous to interpret, but does, nonetheless, seem to be more specific in its reference: the alignments of Neolithic stone monuments taken as evidence for astronomical knowledge. Astro-archaeology has a long history in the discipline, going back to eighteenth-century Antiquarians, but until recently it was discredited in most academic circles (Michell 1977; Thorpe 1983). A retired Scottish professor of engineering, Alexander Thom, published a book in 1967 in which he argued that British megaliths were constructed on a system of geometry and astronomical observation employing a 16-month calendar, and he backed his ideas up with detailed surveys and mathematical calculations (Thom 1967; Figure 3.2). Thom's interpretations were never fully accepted, but he did make the idea of astronomical knowledge in prehistory hard to ignore. It is now largely accepted that many Neolithic monuments do incorporate alignments that indicate knowledge of astronomical phenomena such as summer and winter solstices and equinoxes (see Ruggles 1988). For example, at the Irish megalithic Passage Grave of Newgrange there is a slit in the roof above the entrance which, on the winter solstice, is positioned so that the light from the rising sun lights up the far end of the chamber (O'Kelly 1982: 123–4). In effect, the chamber is thus lit by the Sun only once a year, and this must have been known by people at the time, and probably exploited in ritual practice.

The question is whether it was built in that way or not. This is much harder to argue, but the fact that similar astronomical phenomena can be linked to many other megaliths suggests, perhaps, certain forethought in the construction, especially with regard to orientation. To argue coincidence in all cases may, thus, stretch credibility. However, even if planned, such alignments do not necessarily demonstrate the existence of a time-reckoning system; it would be enough to be aware of the occurrence of an event such as the winter solstice and to indicate or mark it in the construction of a monument and through the recurrence of rites

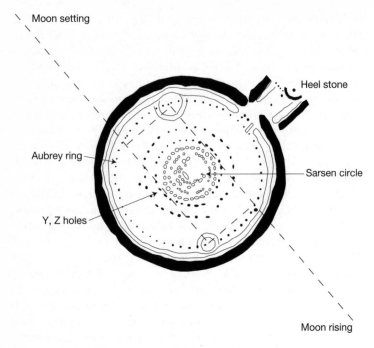

Figure 3.2 Thom's interpretation of the astronomical system implicit in the organization of Stonehenge.

Source: Adapted from Thom and Thom 1978.

associated with that monument at the time. It is the difference between making astronomical observations and actually possessing an astronomical theory or 'science' (Thorpe 1983; Mackie 1988). As with the Palaeolithic bone objects, the evidence only really suggests time indication and not time-reckoning. As a final example of possible time-reckoning in the past, I want to look at the emergence of clocks in Western European society between the fourteenth and eighteenth centuries. This may seem a strange example to take, but in many ways the point is to prove how a familiar object may have once had different temporal associations, and that even clocks may largely have been used as time indication rather than time-reckoning.

Clocks, one would think, are the prime example of the material culture of time-reckoning. They use a regular system of hours and minutes for each day which, by any definition, exemplifies time-reckoning. Certainly, the invention and construction of clocks does presuppose a time-reckoning system – I would not deny this, indeed, such a system is older than clocks and can be seen in sundials, for example. However, what I would suggest is that for most people in Medieval and early Modern Europe, the clock was not *used* as part of a time-reckoning system but primarily as time indication (Lucas 1995; also see Landes 1983). Clocks in the form of public church and tower clocks became fairly widespread from the fourteenth century in European towns and cities and, until the mid-eighteenth century, this was most people's experience of clocks. It was only in the later eighteenth and nineteenth centuries that domestic or interior clocks became at all common in middle-class and, later, working-class homes, as well as inside public rooms such as taverns or workshops. It was only at this time, it has been suggested, that using clocks as time-reckoning developed among the majority of the population. Prior to that time, clocks were simply used as time indication.

The difference can, perhaps, be shown by looking more closely at the design of clocks. First, an important aspect of the Medieval tower clocks was the presence of a striking mechanism – i.e. a gong that struck a bell. Indeed, the word 'clock' in many languages is the same as the word for bell (e.g. French: *cloche*; Latin: *clocca*). For many people, it was the sound of the bell striking that indicated a certain time, rather than people actually reading the clock face to see what time it was. Indeed, some tower clocks seem to have solely consisted of the mechanism and a bell, with no dial at all, such as at Ghent. Bells had a much longer history as time indicators in European culture, being an important part of both monastic and urban life, and used to mark events such as daily Mass or festivals (North 1975; Cipolla 1967). The use of clocks with bells largely continued this tradition, but perhaps also extended it to mark and control labour (Le Goff 1980). The key thing, however, is that clocks in Medieval and early Modern Europe, for most people, did not represent a time-reckoning system but simply time indication. The difference is, while most people responded to the clock, particularly the bell, they did not necessarily *read* it. Only those who made the clock and who controlled its use may be said to have perceived clocks as time-reckoning systems, and it was precisely this difference which perhaps made them suitable tools of power.

Nevertheless, reading clocks is something that did develop among the mass population, and this process probably started to take place during the eighteenth century. This is evident in the gradual and widespread appearance of domestic or interior clocks at this time, and also changes in the design of the clock face (Lucas 1995). In particular, from the eighteenth century, the way time is marked and divided on the clock face goes through various stages of development – at first, there are increasing subdivisions of the hour with just an hour hand, and then after the mid-eighteenth century, a switch to two main divisions, the hour and the minute with two hands. These changes can be said to relate to different ways of reading the time and, perhaps, marking an awareness of smaller divisions of time than previously. It is no coincidence that these changes coincided with changes in the industrial organization of labour and the role clocks played in factory production (Thompson 1967). However, perhaps what it also shows is that enabling the mass of people to read time, meant they also internalized a new time-consciousness that went with it. In other words, the widespread use of clocks in the Modern period as time-reckoning rather than time indication as in the Middle Ages, was related to a new ideology of time perception relating to work discipline.

Clocks can still be used as time indications rather than time-reckoning (e.g. alarm clocks), and this discussion was just meant to show that clocks were not necessarily always used as part of time-reckoning. Indeed, in all the examples of this section, I have looked at possible cases of time-reckoning in the past and raised doubts over their interpretation. None of this is meant to argue that time-reckoning systems did not exist, either in prehistory or Medieval Europe; only that it is often hard to demonstrate. Moreover, it may show that for archaeology, the question of time indication is, perhaps, both more fruitful and more interesting. Indeed, it is really when archaeology leaves the realm of trying to recover evidence of time-reckoning and explores more general issues of temporal perception in the past and its relation to social practice that the most rewarding studies are to be found. Even for past societies with proper time-reckoning systems such as the Maya or Egyptian Kingdoms, these systems are created and used in relation to specific practices, and whether a culture uses time-reckoning systems or more open time indication, it is the way these are linked to social practice that is most important in terms of understanding the society. We have already glimpsed this in the example of clocks in European culture, but the same can be done for any period in the past.

Social memory and social reproduction

Whether or not we can discern evidence of time-marking in the archaeological record, the evidence for time-consciousness through social practice is generally much more common and accessible. The link between them has been most usefully articulated through the concept of social or collective memory – that is, how societies remember (Connerton 1989; Halbwachs 1992). Connerton's study provides a key text here in so far as it is tied into the problem of the transmission of knowledge in non-literate societies. He focuses on the *act* of transmission and, specifically, on two types of act: commemorative ceremonies and bodily practices. I will discuss commemorative practices later in the next section, but for the moment it is his discussion of bodily practices that is most relevant here. Connerton observes that a central part of social memory and the transmission of cultural knowledge is associated with repeated, habitual actions such as learning to hunt, learning to make pottery etc. Such memory is transmitted either through what he calls inscribing or incorporating practices. Inscribing practices rely on external information storage (or artificial memory systems – see above), such as writing and other notational systems. A time-reckoning system would probably require such inscription. Incorporating practice, on the other hand, relies primarily on actions of the body to transmit information, and includes gestures, manners or etiquette but also ceremonies or rituals in which the body 'performs' the information.

The reproduction of society is largely dependent on repetitive incorporating practices, and in non-literate societies, wholly dependent. To take the example of archaeological excavation, no one would suggest a student should learn how to do this from a manual or text book; that is why there are field schools, 'practicals' and usually minimum field experience requirements. Like most other practices, the transmission of knowledge in excavation comes through the incorporating practices of actually working on site, and the inscription practices pertaining to manuals, though important, cannot substitute for this. In the context of interpreting the past, this is a very useful recognition to make (Rowlands 1993). Practices evident in the archaeological record will convey something of the nature of social memory and cultural transmission simply because most practices tend to be repetitive and incorporative. The trick is to examine the nature of that repetition and incorporation and how it relates to social memory and temporal perception more generally. The best way to demonstrate this is through some examples.

Perhaps one of the most obvious ways in which social memory is implicated in practice is in developmental cycles, of individuals or households. In most societies, individuals go through various life stages – for example, child to adult, single to married; usually these are in several stages (age grades or strata) and marked by rites of passage with the person associated with a particular group of contemporaries who pass through each stage together (age set or cohort; see Kertzer and Keith 1984). For example, the field school or training dig can be seen as an initiation rite, it marks the passage of the student into becoming a field archaeologist, after which, if they continue, they will eventually join the 'elders' of this practice. Most of what they learn will be gained in the presence of these 'elders' and in the same way, these former students will eventually provide the context for the next generation of would-be field archaeologists. What applies to the individual also applies to groups, particularly households where the changing composition of a household will create similar developmental cycles (Goody 1958). As household members age or die, marry and have children, so the household goes through a cycle of growth and shrinkage. Moreover, what young individuals learn in the domestic context as they experience it from their own perspective, so they reproduce when they establish their own household, consciously or not. The temporal structure to a household is intimately associated with the temporal structure of its individuals and their memory is what recreates the household from generation to generation.

Archaeological studies of these cycles are not common but they have been attempted. The individual life cycle has not really been explicitly addressed as far as I am aware, though there have been various studies that attempt a more general association of status with age on the one hand (e.g. Shennan 1975) and, on the other, studies that focus on certain life stages, specifically childhood (e.g. Sofaer Deverenski 2000). Surprisingly, household cycles seem to have received rather more attention, but still are hardly abundant; one of the first papers to highlight their potential was an ethnoarchaeological study (Lane 1987). Archaeological studies of the household developmental cycle come from the Americas (Tourtellot 1988; Goodman 1999), but there are few from prehistoric Europe. Ruth Tringham discusses the notion of the household cycle in broader symbolic terms (Tringham 1991), while Bradley has looked at the developmental cycle of Neolithic (LBK) long houses of central Europe, and makes an interesting connection between their abandonment and the development of the long barrow tradition (Bradley 2002: 24). Bradley's study was influenced by an excellent study of late prehistoric household cycles in the Netherlands, which is worth summarizing, as it exemplifies the key ideas here (Gerritsen 1999).

In the southern Netherlands during the Late Bronze Age and Iron Age, settlements tend to be fairly short-lived, often being abandoned after a single phase of occupation – unlike later periods, when longer-lived and more stable settlements predominate. Conventionally, this has been explained by the natural lifespan of timber buildings and soil depletion; however, drawing on ethnographic cases, Gerritsen suggests that such abandonment should be seen in social terms of the household cycle – that the biography or life cycle of the house follows that of the social unit occupying it (Figure 3.3). Constructing a new house was symbolic of the formation of a new unit – perhaps at the marriage of a couple or the birth of their first child, and was often accompanied by foundation deposits. As the family unit grew with new children being born and growing up, so the house aged – parts were repaired or renovated, the house may even have been extended. Finally, when the head of the household died, or its members left to set up new households of their own, so the house may have been abandoned and left to decay, its natural life-span coming to an end around the same time as the household unit – i.e. one genera-tion. New houses are usually built far away from earlier houses which may remain abandoned or used as a focus of ritual activity – either way, there is greater emphasis of transience and discon-tinuity. Towards the end of the Iron Age this pattern changes, as new houses tend to be built adjacent to, or even over, earlier houses, suggesting greater continuity and, possibly, the formation of durable lineages and the association of farmsteads with ancestral places.

However, it is not just life cycles, whether of individuals or households, which display temporal structure – any regular social practice that helps to reproduce society should include time as part of its organization. A study of Bronze Age burial rites in Britain has shown that social memory played a key role in the location of burials, specifically in burial mounds or barrows which had been used as places of interment over long periods of time (Mizoguchi 1993). Looking at the order of multiple burials as well as the position, age and sex of the person, Mizoguchi found that very specific memories must have been retained of *who* was buried *where* and in *what position*. Thus, he found that adult males tended to be the primary burial and adult females and juveniles secondary and that the secondary burial either repeated or mirrored the orientation of the primary burial. This recurrent pattern was taken to indicate that detailed memories were retained of burials, possibly by only a section of the community, but more generally,

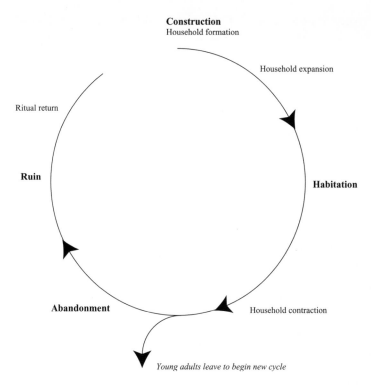

Figure 3.3 The household cycle in the later prehistoric Netherlands.
Source: Adapted from Gerritsen 1999.

it also illustrates how the continuation of a practice over a long period of time was sustained through social memory. A similar case can be cited for ritual foundation deposits associated with buildings in Chaco canyon in the American Southwest (Kovacik 1998), where it was argued that repeated deposits of specific animal species – carnivores and birds of prey – with certain structures indicates an active collective memory which helped to sustain links to the past and the reproduction of communal identity. Van Dyke provides an even broader survey of the role of memory in Chacoan society, looking at a number of strategies where collective memory is exploited to legitimate certain forms of new inequality (van Dyke 2003).

All of these examples raise the question of continuity or repetition of cultural practice over a long period, and rather than assume this simply 'happens' by reference to some vague sense of tradition, they actually examine the nature of the practice and what it implies in terms of social memory. But how can such an analysis increase our understanding of past perceptions of time? At the moment, all we have is the recognition of the temporal structure of practice – how does this enlighten us as to temporal perception? Mizoguchi suggests that the repetitive nature of the practice he describes in Bronze Age burial might indicate a cyclical conception of time, but this seems a little vague. Similarly, Thorpe's examination of the social significance of the use of astronomical observations in monuments is regarded as indicative of a cyclical view of time (Thorpe 1983: 3–4). The use of typologies of time conceptions such as Gurevich's eight chronotypes (Gurevich 1964), or the more common ethnographic pair of linear and cyclical time, have been used in archaeology but infrequently. A good example is Douglas Bailey's discussion of chronotypes in Bulgarian prehistory; he argues that both linear and cyclical perceptions of time are evident during the Neolithic and Early Bronze Age, but that during the Chalcolithic, a tension arose between them which resulted in the predominance of linear chronotype (Bailey 1993).

Bailey argued that seasonal patterns of agriculture, settlement occupation and early burial ritual (in houses) designate a cyclical conception of time, while practices such as record keeping (e.g. pottery stamps and seals), later burial ritual (in formal cemeteries) and the build-up of tells, suggest a cumulative or linear conception of time. During the Chalcolithic, those practices associated with a linear conception intensified, resulting in what he calls a 'chronotypic tension' and, ultimately, in the dominance of a linear perception of time. This is an interesting attempt to actually examine temporal perceptions through practice, but it suffers from an over-simplification and reliance on a 'temporal typology' of chronotypes. At the end of the chapter I will discuss this issue of chronotypes further, chiefly in terms of the opposition of linear and cyclical time. For the present, it is more constructive to find other ways in which temporal perceptions might be disclosed in the archaeological record.

One consideration is to look at the temporal meaning of continuity; does it, for example, suggest conservatism and, by implication, a sense of timelessness? If continuity is intentional, then is it intended to create a sense of continuity with the past, and if so, does this mean a practice that is primarily oriented to the past or one that ignores the passage of time, perhaps claiming to be eternal? Conversely, if another practice seems to undergo rapid or relatively rapid change, does this imply a future-oriented practice, or one that seeks to break with the past? These comments are not to suggest a new way of classifying a society by a simple bipolar attitude to time so much as defining a particular practice. Any society might contain a mixture of conservative and innovative practices, and perhaps the key task is to map these out and see what practices incorporate what temporal perceptions. This will give a much richer and deeper representation of the cultural perception of time in that society than imposing overall chronotypes. For example, in our society there is a very innovative core to our casual dress, but at the same time, other aspects of clothing are relatively stable and conservative, such as uniforms. The relative innovation or conservatism of these two types of clothing is probably linked to implicit conceptions of time, with uniforms being associated with authority legitimated by a stability and continuity with the past, while casual dress is more closely aligned with individual choice and an ability to transcend the past. This is not to argue for an opposition between static and changing practices, rather, that practices may change at different *rates*, and the relation between conservatism and innovation will always be a relative and plural one. This observation is particularly interesting given the discussion in Chapter 1, for it suggests that the same approach to looking at explanations of cultural change will also have implications for temporal perception in the past.

The past in the past

The previous section mostly discussed ways in which continuity is maintained through social memory and the implications for this in terms of perceptions of time. Equally, where a radical break with the past was intended through a transformation or cessation of certain cultural practices, this too had implications for temporal perception. But in both cases, the perception involved is largely one that is contained within living memory; what of distant times, beyond such memory – how did past societies view their own past? This is the subject of this final section and it is worth returning to Connerton's study as a useful guide (Connerton 1989). Recall that Connerton made a distinction between bodily practices and commemorative practices, the former primarily associated with habitual action and social reproduction. By commemorative practices, in contrast, he meant practices that intentionally recollect the past, often involving re-enactment of narrative events from the past. The distinction is largely mirrored by the philosophical distinction between habitual memory and recollective memory – i.e. the often implicit or unconscious memory we have of how to do something such as ride a bicycle on the one hand, and, on the other, the more explicit, conscious memory of recollecting events such as 'that bicycle trip in France in the summer of 1996'.

The examples in the previous section largely examined social memory as habitual memory, the transmission of cultural knowledge through bodily practices which help to reproduce (or potentially transform) the social structure. These practices had a temporal structure which, it is argued, have implications for temporal perception, but this was only loosely suggested and, indeed, these temporal perceptions may have been as unconscious as the actions themselves. In terms of a more explicit time-consciousness however, it is social recollective memory that is most informative; it is here that a society's own sense of time will be most evident. Such recollection, moreover, is not confined to language, written or spoken; indeed, the use of ceremonies and material culture is a dominant part of social recollection, through ritual practices which intentionally engage with the past. For example, the common presence of war memorials and commemorative days in our own society play a major role in remembering the two world wars of the twentieth century and the ideology surrounding them (Tarlow 1999: 147–70; Winter 1995). Such rituals probably play a less important role in our society, though, than others, not simply because of the role writing has, but specifically the role of history as a discipline and its inscriptive practice of books.

In archaeology, an early paper by Horst discusses the 'attitude of prehistoric man towards his history' (Horst 1954), and while there has been other occasional interest (especially outside Anglo-American archaeology), it is only recently that it has become a more popular topic. A whole issue of the journal *World Archaeology* was recently devoted to exploring this theme, specifically focusing on the re-use of monuments (1998, volume 30: 1). In the first paper, Gosden and Lock invoke the anthropological distinction between mythical and genealogical time (see above) and argue, using the example of later prehistoric Berkshire, that these different perceptions of time are expressed in the ways sites are used/reused over time (Gosden and Lock 1998). For example, they suggest that the Late Bronze Age hillfort of Ram's Hill, which shows three phases of similar enclosure separated by periods of abandonment, indicates a period when long genealogical histories were prominent, social memory allowing continuity in genealogical time. In contrast, during the Early Iron Age, the activity on sites such as Segsbury was much more intense and rapid, indicating shorter genealogical histories. Finally, sites such as Uffington hillfort reveal that mythical histories must have been at work as this site incorporates remains from the Neolithic through to the Roman period.

How far such generalized oppositions, such as the distinction between genealogical and mythical history, work is open to debate (cf. Bailey's paper on linear and cyclical time in the Bulgarian Neolithic discussed above). Certainly, they have been criticized within anthropology and I discuss such dichotomies in the concluding section of this chapter. Interestingly though, even in modern nation states, a similar vernacular dichotomy may operate if commemorative events are anything to go by. Zerubavel, in a study of a large sample of national calendars found that national holidays tended to commemorate events either in the very recent past or in the very distant, near mythical past – the one often associated with the formation of the country as a nation state and the other with ancient religious beliefs (Zerubavel 2003: 31–4). Certainly, in this respect, it is interesting to consider how our perception of temporal distance can be affected by such dualities; in Chapter 1, I showed a figure of the ancient Egyptian chronology (Figure 1.2) – as Zerubavel observes, we unconsciously associate all phases of this chronology as much closer together than any part of it is to modern Egypt – yet the Late Period is, in fact, closer in chronological time to the present day than it is to the First Dynasty. Such temporal perceptions of near and distant time are clearly unrelated to strict chronology but, rather, to cultural affiliation, and may, indeed, be part of a deeper division between history and prehistory (see Chapter 5).

Another volume to come out recently is *Archaeologies of Memory* (van Dyke and Alcock 2003) which includes a number of studies of social memory in an archaeological context from various periods and regions. However, the most detailed study on social recollective memory in archaeology to date is undoubtedly Richard Bradley's book *The Past in Prehistoric Societies* (2002). This is a rich source of ideas and examples on how past societies engaged with *their* past, through rituals and commemorative practices. Bradley sums it up well:

> There is no doubt that people would have been aware of the built fabric of their own past in the landscapes in which they lived. Even if they had chosen to ignore it, it would have still posed a problem. At the same time, they would have encountered some of the concealed deposits of artifacts . . . They would have found these in the process of clearing the land, while opening new graves in older burial mounds or in rebuilding their settlements, and again they would have faced a similar challenge. Like

archaeologists . . . they would have been forced to use these scraps of ancient material culture to understand their place in the world.

(Bradley 2002: 13–14)

So how can archaeology explore these themes? Quite simply, any aspect of the archaeological record that would seem to indicate some reference to an earlier part of that record might be interpreted in this way. The strength of the interpretation will, of course, depend on the plausibility of the reference. For example, re-use of old monuments, the curation and re-use of artefacts, even imitation of 'old' material culture, suggest that some explicit reference is being made to the past. Howard Williams discusses the frequent re-use of old monuments in the location of Anglo-Saxon burials – typically around one quarter of all burials of this period occur on older monuments, chiefly round barrows (Williams 1998). He suggests this can be seen as part of a general strategy of appropriating the past by incoming settlers to legitimate their presence in the land, but this interpretation is given a more interesting twist by subsequent developments. In the seventh century AD, an emergent elite started to construct their own, new barrows, which took this appropriation one stage further – it suggested that this new elite were, in fact, descendants of the original barrow builders. Here, we see two key material strategies that reference the past – re-use and imitation to create historical links for a new immigrant population.

Even on everyday settlements, not just monuments, such practices can inform us about past people's attitudes to their past. Thus, in a paper on the prehistoric settlement of Lepenski Vir in south-east Europe, Borić suggests several strategies were employed by the occupants to engage with the temporality of their settlement, which included altering, moving and referencing traces or remains of earlier buildings (Borić 2003). Just as we build a visitors' centre around Stonehenge, display its finds in museum cases, and even reproduce prehistoric artefacts for sale, so past societies in their own way engaged with Stonehenge. Many of these ways may be lost, but some survive. Indeed, given the lack of writing and the concept of history as we understand it, most such interactions in the past are likely to have been directly engaged with the remains themselves and, therefore, leave some material trace. Even the general nature of activities might give an indication of how a society perceives its past; for example, does building next to or on top of earlier remains (but without necessarily damaging them) suggest a perception that stresses continuity with the past, where in fact the present and the past are not considered distinct? What did it mean to live on a tell in the prehistoric Near East, or a farm mound in Medieval North Atlantic in these terms? Conversely, does cutting into a former monument or site, modifying it, mixing the past and present, signal a greater sense of a break with the past? Archaeology is driven by this kind of process – digging up sites – and it does it precisely because it feels so alienated from the past it is trying to recover, the past as a foreign country (Lowenthal 1985).

A common theme of many studies of the role of collective memory is the connection to power – the use of the past to legitimate the present. Much of this draws inspiration from an important series of historical essays on the invention of tradition in the past 200 years, and the idea that societies *create* traditions or a past in order to make the present seem natural or proper (Hobsbawm and Ranger 1983). Elites who exploit monuments or traces of the past to make a connection with the status quo in the present, provide an authority that draws on the collective memory of the subaltern population; it is a powerful ideology. However, the flipside to this is iconoclasm – the destruction of traces of the past in order to sever any material links that might challenge the authority of an elite. Forgetting is as important a strategy as remembering (Forty and Küchler 1999). Bradley's book provides many interesting case studies, but one is particularly interesting because it draws on the relation between remembering and forgetting: 'the statues that moved' (Bradley 2002: 36–41). Several Neolithic burial chambers along the Atlantic fringe of Europe (e.g. France, Spain and Portugal) have carved motifs on the stonework incorporated into their structure, and in many cases these stones were originally part of free-standing stelae or menhirs. Indeed, in one case (in Brittany), fragments of the *same* decorated menhir occur in two different tombs, three kilometres apart. Moreover, recent excavations have uncovered empty sockets from where such menhirs have been uplifted. All in all, there is now compelling evidence that menhirs were often levelled or broken up, and sometimes re-used in tombs, either whole or as fragments. This has been interpreted as an attempt to erase the past through destruction – i.e. iconoclasm. However, Bradley suggests that the destruction of menhirs was actually a way of remembering – by forgetting. He draws on Küchler's ethnographic analysis of the Malangan ritual where effigies are built to contain the souls of deceased people; the gradual decay of these effigies gives material form to the gradual forgetting of the person (Küchler 1987). Thus, there is never an intention to have a permanent memorial, rather only a temporary one whose eventual destruction mirrors the destruction of the person, but one which, in the process, will acquire public renown. Bradley suggests a similar scenario with the menhirs because of the close association they have with tombs, with menhirs commemorating individuals. Like the bones of the individual, the menhir would have eventually been broken up and incorporated into tombs, and these acts would have memorialized the deceased while, at the same time, creating the context for their gradual forgetting and dispersal into the more general social category of ancestors. In this way, menhirs act as key devices for translating the present into the past and, perhaps, mediating genealogical time and ancestral time.

Bradley's study, and many others, draws on the re-use of monuments and sites to explore issues of time and social memory, but artefacts also provide insights. A final example brings us to a more recent time of Medieval and early Modern Period and the concept of patina. Patina is that quality of an object that indicates age, the signs of longevity – gloss on old wood, spots on old silver or pewter, general wear and tear. In Medieval and early Modern England, the patina of household possessions was an important symbol of the family's status and honour, chiefly aristocratic families but more generally any household that owned what might be called heirlooms (McCracken 1990: 31–43). In the context of

Elizabethan England, the patina on objects was a key characteristic which separated 'new' from 'old' money, for status came not simply from wealth but from standing wealth – reference was often made to the 'five generation rule', which was the number of generations required before a household could be said to have crossed the line from *nouveaux riches* to gentility. Since new wealth, by necessity, was usually signalled by new material goods, patina was pivotal in determining, at a glance, the status of a family. This was not necessarily meant to exclude people from entering the gentry; merely to slow the process down and control it. Of course, this symbolism could be subverted by buying up another family's heirlooms, but this must have been rare given the shame that would accompany revelation. The whole symbolism of patina was tied up with honour as much as status and its association with family history.

This symbolism of patina, of course, remains with us today but in a completely different form; today, patina is commodified, as we can purchase old objects just like new objects – the only association they have is an abstract one of the 'antique'. Indeed, it is perhaps only in its commodified form that 'faking' patina becomes a major practice. Unlike Elizabethan England, then, patina now signifies age as a commodity, not as family history. This change in the symbolism of patina occurred in the later eighteenth century as the so-called 'consumer revolution' swept England (McKendrick *et al.* 1982). Suddenly, wealth and status were marked by new material culture, and rather than patina or age acting to signal status, now it was novelty – the latest design, the latest fashion helped to accrue status. We can explore this concept archaeologically through the role of specific objects such as tablewares. Given that much more research has been done in North America than Britain, I will use a study from eighteenth-century Virginia to exemplify this transition, although it is probably equally applicable to England (Martin 1989).

One of the curious things about the archaeological record of the early Modern period, particularly the seventeenth and eighteenth centuries, is the lack of a major type of artefact used for the table in homes and taverns everywhere: pewter. This material is not perishable, though admittedly it does degrade. Yet, it is hardly ever found, despite being a major component of domestic tableware assemblages in the form of plates, tankards and other items, as probate inventories testify (ibid.). A large part of the reason for this is undoubtedly due to two characteristics: its durability and its recyclability. If you drop it, at most it acquires a dent, and if it starts to look too battered or is no longer wanted, it can be sold for scrap or recast. For this reason, it makes for a good material as tableware. Yet, towards the end of the eighteenth century and into the first decades of the nineteenth century, its role was completely supplanted by ceramics, which were eminently breakable and non-recyclable. Why?

Some reasons undoubtedly relate to cost – the new industrial refined earthenwares such as creamwares and pearlwares, were vastly cheaper (a third to quarter of the cost). Also, the widespread adoption of drinking hot beverages such as tea and coffee made pewter impractical. Pewter was also limited in terms of its decorative potential, unlike the 'white canvas' of pottery (ibid.). However, most of these are largely contingent reasons to the larger issue of the changing nature of consumption. We may not think of pewter in the same league as 'family silver', but in the seventeenth century it certainly carried connotations of status and wealth, and was often on display in homes. Moreover, as Ann Smart Martin points out, it took quite a long time for the introduction of mass-produced ceramics to replace pewter in homes, a lag that cannot be due to financial reasons (ibid.). I think the lag can be related to the changing role of patina and the changing nature of consumption as McCracken has discussed (McCracken 1990). Pewter, unlike ceramics, carried 'patina' *because* of its durability, and thus it had the power to invoke family history. Ceramics, though they are potentially durable and repairable, more importantly, are also more disposable and cheaply replaceable. Ceramics were a much better material for the new style of consumption than pewter because of these qualities, and this is why they replaced pewter as the primary element of tableware. Moreover, this transition took place first among the wealthiest sections of society – as would be expected, even though ceramics were *cheaper* than pewter (Martin 1989). The explosion of ceramic tablewares in the archaeological record in the late eighteenth and early nineteenth centuries tells us not just about new patterns of consumption, but whole new ways of perceiving the world, which included time. The notion of tablewares having family history, that every time you sat down to eat you were also using objects with personal historical meaning, was completely altered by the replacement of pewter by ceramics.

Both examples suggest that the nature of material culture, and particularly its temporal properties, reveal information about a society's perception of time. How a society creates links with the past through ceremony, how it engages with the *aging* of material culture, provide windows into its perception of earlier times. In ending this chapter, I want to summarize the main points and also return to some broader themes about the social perception of time.

Temporal oppositions

I began this chapter by showing how time as a concept was a social category of thought and that although time may be something all societies experience in similar ways, nevertheless, how it is articulated and represented is culturally specific. Different societies mark time in different ways, and much of this marking is linked to the temporal organization of social practice – such as seasonal rites or tasks. Indeed, the temporal structure of practice highlights the key role of social memory, and provides an important way in to understanding social perception of time in terms of continuity and change. More generally, social memory also plays a key role in commemorative rites which reveal how a society consciously engages with its past.

Throughout the chapter, I have tried to emphasize, either through example or assertion, that social representations of time are very much multiple – not single or dual, even within any society. Nevertheless, it is difficult to avoid oppositions, not just in discussing time but any concept. Indeed, I have drawn on oppositions, such as the distinction between time indication and time-reckoning, or habitual memory and recollective memory.

I do see these oppositions as useful ways of discussing the topic, but I would not want to overplay them. But there are several oppositions that I find more harmful than useful, especially if they are used to dichotomize societies or practices. In this respect, I would single out two: abstract/substantial time and linear/cyclical time. Sometimes these oppositions reinforce each other, sometimes not, but I want to suggest that neither of them is very helpful.

The distinction between linear and cyclical time can be argued to be spurious, since to perceive linearity in time depends on repetition or periodicity and, conversely, to recognize cycles presupposes directional movement. How can we talk about aging, or the duration of an event, without marking it in some way through repetitive units such as minutes, hours, days or years? It does not matter that these units are even regular, nor are they specific to Western time-reckoning systems. For example, consider the story related by Lawrence Durrell of the islanders of Cyprus marking the length of journeys by how many cigarettes they smoked on the way (Durrell 1957). The journey is linear but to recognize its linearity requires marking it through cycles of repeated events, in this case, 'smokes'. Conversely, how can we talk about cyclical or repetitive events such as birthdays or even cigarette 'breaks' without thinking of the duration between these events as a linear movement of time. The two terms are, then, very much interdependent and, certainly as metaphors for different kinds of time perception (i.e. chronotypes), should be avoided.

Similarly, the distinction between abstract and substantial time is often associated with the distinction between modern or Western and pre-modern/non-Western perception of time; but this is based on a misguided comprehension of our own temporal experiences. For example, modern/Western time is often described as abstract and scientific, while non-Western time is socially concrete, embedded in daily life. But this is clearly a false characterization, as most of our personal experience of time in the West is just as deeply embedded in our social life – we perceive time in terms of leisure and work, meals, and events such as Christmas (e.g. see Zerubavel 1981). Even our clock time is deeply socialized – the phrase 'it's Friday, it's five o'clock' is not just an abstract temporal location – it is loaded with social meaning. In this, therefore, we are no different from any other society; our so-called abstract time is merely one aspect of our temporal perception which we use in specific contexts – namely, science. Conversely, other societies that use time-reckoning systems might equally perceive time as 'abstract' in some contexts. Anthropologists and archaeologists who claim that Western time is abstract are clearly only thinking about time in terms of their discipline and not their daily lives.

In short, time is multiple, not singular. In our society, as in all societies past and present, time is perceived in many different ways according to the context, and it is much more useful to try to understand the specific temporalities or 'temporalizing' that are involved in social practice than to classify time into chrono-types – such as linear/cyclical or genealogical/mythical. The term 'chronotype', however, can carry different meanings; in a general sense, it refers simply to social constructions of time and their variability historically and culturally (Bender and Wellberg 1991; also see Gosden 1994). In this sense, this whole chapter has been about chronotypes. However, in archaeology it seems to be used mostly in the more specific sense of typologies of time perception such as linear/cyclical etc. (e.g. Gurevich 1964), and it is this restricted meaning that I find problematic. Indeed, it is more productive when looking at past people's perception of time to think in terms of associated temporal concepts rather than time itself, even though these may be equally oppositional: remembering and forgetting, old and new, continuity and change. Such oppositions provide a conceptual dynamic with which to address the archaeological record and are more methodological than substantive. They are not intended to create static typologies but dynamic narratives and are tools for uncovering the diversity and multiplicity of temporal experience.

4

CASE STUDY

The life and times of a Roman jar

In this chapter I want to present a case study that illustrates many of the themes I have been discussing in the previous three chapters. This is not necessarily an easy task as some material and contexts are better for discussing some issues more than others, so this study will by no means cover everything. Indeed, I have deliberately chosen a rather ordinary subject in the hope that the reader will appreciate how the concept of time in archaeology can be perceived and addressed with any archaeological material. Many of the other cases studies quoted or discussed elsewhere in this book may certainly provide better examples of specific themes in relation to time, and the reader is encouraged to read these first hand. Thus, in this chapter, I simply want to dissect a 'typical' archaeological example under a temporal lens, to expose as fully as possible how the concept of time is implicated in all stages of the archaeological process and interpretation of the past.

During excavations of a Romano-British settlement in eastern England in 2000, a cremation cemetery was found, and one burial in particular was found during the later stages of the investigation (Figure 4.1; Lucas and Whittaker 2001). The technical description of the cremation as it appears in the excavation report is as follows:

An unurned burial was associated with two flagons and a jar placed on top of the cremated bone. The jar contained a few fragments of burnt bone and it may be that it had tipped over and spilled its contents. All the human bone fragments were well calcined with the exception of some of the skull fragments. Recognisable fragments include skull, pelvis, upper and lower limbs (femur head 39 mm), vertebrae, teeth and phalanges. Although the majority of fragments are adult (possibly female) some immature skull fragments were identified. The largest fragment (skull) is 74 mm. Cremated animal bones also occurred, and included a chicken coracoid, a sheep-sized femur and 12 sheep-sized rib fragments, as well as 133 unidentifiable pieces.

(Dodwell, in Lucas and Whittaker 2001)

One of the vessels in this cremation – the jar that originally held the cremated bone – will be the subject of this chapter. There is nothing special about it – it is like thousands of others – but, like any object, it carries within it multiple temporalities and serves

Figure 4.1 Romano-British cremation from eastern England.

as an exemplar of many of the themes discussed in the previous three chapters. It is for its very ordinariness that I have selected it. The jar, after it had been removed from the ground, was bagged and sent back to the finds room where it was cleaned, re-bagged and catalogued. Jar number 3732 was then examined by a pottery specialist to yield a source and date of manufacture among other things. It was drawn by an illustrator and then placed in a strong cardboard box with other vessels and stored away (Figure 4.2). Here is the technical description of this jar:

> Everted rim jar with burnished acute-lattice (6 sherds, 118 g, 0.90 eves). 9.4 cm tall, rim diameter, 7 cm. The fabric is hard with a sand-tempered grey core and burnished to a smooth bluish finish with acute-lattice decoration. This fabric is very uncommon on the site, in fact this was the only instance. The type probably derives

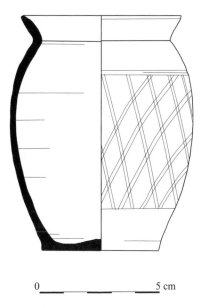

0 ____ ____ ____ 5 cm

Figure 4.2 Jar 3732.

from Essex, and can be classed as a BB2-type ware. The vessel form is a cooking jar and dates to the mid 2nd century AD.

(Monteil, in Lucas and Whittaker 2001)

So how can we begin to address the question of time through this jar? As always, perhaps, one should begin with chronology – after all, almost without exception, the first question any archaeologist would ask about the jar is its date. Indeed, often this is also the last question.

Conflicting chronologies

The use of ceramics as dating tools is ubiquitous – their stylistic variation with respect to time is widely exploited and, as a quick and effective means of dating a feature or a site, they are perhaps unsurpassed. Yet, it is worth remembering that a vessel – such as this jar – incorporates many chronologies within it, of different scales or resolutions. Thus, jar 3732 can be characterized as:

- Romano-British;
- mid 2nd century;
- Hadrianic-Antonine;
- Phase I;
- earlier than the colluvium.

At least five different chronological systems intersect in the jar: its identification as 'Romano-British' puts it within a broad periodization, after the Iron Age and before the Saxon periods. Its calendrical date of 'mid 2nd century' places it within an absolute (or interval) chronology, while the designation 'Hadrianic-Antonine' aligns it with Roman imperial reigns. Finally, 'Phase I' and 'earlier than the colluvium' place it in a series purely internal to the site. Of course, we usually try to relate each chronology to the other, but this often causes difficulty, especially between absolute/interval and relative/ordinal chronologies. We can relate the calendrical system to the imperial reigns largely because we have written documents and a Roman calendrical system that can all be fairly accurately tied together. However, tying the calendrical system to site phasing, stratigraphy or broad period-ization is much harder, and to avoid the problems caused by two very different systems, we usually decrease the resolution of the calendrical system, perhaps by using a date range or a *circa*. For example, Phase I was estimated to have begun *c*.AD 60, but this *circa* in front of the date indicates ambiguity, despite the very precise year given. How much ambiguity is not stated – it could be up to 10 years in this case. The cremation burial itself, as a stratigraphic event is even more ambiguous and assigned a range in the calendrical chronology of AD 140–180 – an ambiguity of 40 years, even though the burial actually took place in just one year somewhere in that period (and probably just one day in that year). Finally, the periodization is especially interesting because it highlights a potential source of major conflict between two chronological systems.

Historical evidence puts the Roman invasion of Britain at AD 43, and the separation of the provinces of Britain from Rome in AD 410, and thus, conventionally, the Romano-British period covers the span between these very specific dates. However, the precision of the calendrical system does not match the periodization as a whole – certainly, the time spans of the other periods such as the Iron Age, which precedes it, or the Saxon or early Medieval periods which follow, are much less vague – generally anywhere to between a half or whole century. The problem here lies not so much with our ability to fix the dates of a period, so much as the inherent temporal ambiguity of a period; the Iron Age begins *c*.800 BC, but this *circa* indicates not so much ambiguity of accuracy as ambiguity of resolution. The Iron Age as a period operates on a much larger temporal scale than the calendrical system – it is pointless to refine the calendrical dating of the Iron Age to anything less than perhaps half a century, since the Iron Age characterizes larger scale processes that do not operate on the level of years, but decades or more. If this is the case, the same is also true, then, of the Romano-British period; the problem is that the period has been defined by historical documents, which track events at the annual level or less, while most of the data and archaeological interpretation works on very different timescales. The 'problem' of the end of Roman Britain – i.e. how society changed after the departure of the Roman legions in Britain – is largely a fictitious problem of two incommensurable chronologies.

This is not to deny that the fifth century witnessed major changes in society – but the precision of the date of AD 410 and the associated historical events may cause us to over-emphasize and seek a more rapid change than we would otherwise normally do. For example, the production and, certainly, use of Roman pottery probably continued well into the fifth century AD. Moreover, the Roman period is the only period in English archaeology that has special extra periods to designate this ambiguity – called the Sub-Roman period for after AD 410 and the Late Pre-Roman Iron Age (LPRIA), for the century before AD 43. That we have created these short transitional periods is more to do with the incompatible resolutions of two chronologies than any special problems of the Roman period. Other periods do have similar problems, especially when it comes to the use of radiocarbon dates; for example, consider the debate surrounding the Meadowcroft Rockshelter and the advent of human migration into North America discussed in Chapter 1. Similar 'problems' have arisen and, predictably, could arise in other contexts – for example, if archaeologists found an object on a site radiocarbon dated to a particular time, conventional periodization would put the object much later – e.g. pottery on a Mesolithic site in England.

Fortunately, the jar that is the subject of this chapter falls well within the Roman period and so this is not an issue that will occupy us any further. Nevertheless, similar issues will potentially arise between any two chronological systems and it is one that we need to be aware of when dealing with questions of dating. Perhaps the most common revolves around the original dating of the pottery type in the first place. How do we know the jar is mid-second century in the first place? It does not have a date marked on it, and there are no historical documents that tell us when this type was produced. The answer comes from association with other dated finds – ultimately, coins. The type of vessel that jar 3732 can be classed as, has been found in other deposits all over the country, and in association with other pottery or coins that have enabled the construction of a date span for the type (AD 120–160). In some cases, the dating may come predominantly from other pottery that was, in turn, dated by coins or other historical evidence – such as the imported fine ware. Obviously, the chain of association becomes weaker the further removed the dating is from an original absolute date – just as the prehistoric chron-ologies of Western Europe broke down the further away they were from historic sources (see Chapter 1, Figure 1.1). Thus, there is a potential problem of circularity here, for the date assigned to any object by a type series is usually not strictly the date of its produc-tion, but an *aggregate date of its deposition* (Millett 1987: 101). Usually, since types are dated from a wide range of contexts from different sites and carefully selected, the dates are fairly reliable, but problems can arise. Moreover, the danger is that once a chron-ology is created it is seldom checked, and anomalies can easily be overlooked. For example, if our jar 3732, dated to AD 120–160 was found in a context dated by other finds to AD 200–220, we could simply say it was curated and deposited much later; if the pot was just present as a few sherds, we could even say it is just residual. If the context was dated much earlier, however – say AD 90, then we may have more problems; a single sherd could be intrusive but not a whole pot. In this case, we may revise our original dating of the context, and even claim the other objects that provided the date were residual or curated, even if they outnumber the one jar dated much later.

Jar 3732 was found with two other vessels, both flagons that typologically date to *c*.AD 140–180 which, since the jar dates to *c*.AD 120–160, points to an overlap of two decades. This suggests all three vessels are more or less contemporary and were regarded as such when they were deposited. There is certainly very little to raise any doubts over the dating here. In some instances, however, the anomalies may grow and be too frequent, and revision to the type chronology is needed. In actual fact, this seems to be the case with the type series to which jar 3732 belongs. This jar falls into

101

a certain typology constructed by Romano-British ceramicists and conventionally incorporates a regular typological progression. It is this type series that enabled the vessel to be dated. The type series was first outlined by John Gillam in the 1950s and, through successive refinements, a definitive sequence for Black Burnished wares was produced (Gillam 1976), with this type – the cooking pot – showing a gradual and even progression of form between the first and fourth centuries AD, based on its occurrence in deposits dated by other finds (Figure 4.3). According to this typology, jar 3732 can be dated approximately to the period AD 120–160. However, the first doubts of a simple progression were expressed by anomalous vessels (Farrar 1981), followed by a detailed reconsideration of the sequence (Holbrook and Bidwell 1991: 88–137). Currently, the variability in forms are seen to be much less neat – and, in fact, rather than a gradual progression, the form exhibits only one major period of change, between c.AD 120–240 where it seems to conform to Gillam's sequence, while on either side of that period, his sequence breaks down.

This question of chronological variability of a form is interesting because the conventional model used by Gillam is very

AD 120–160   AD 160–280   AD 280–370

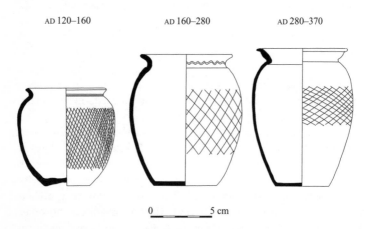

0 _____ 5 cm

Figure 4.3 Type series for Black Burnished ware jars.
Source: Adapted from Gillam 1976.

much based on assumptions of linear temporality – the idea that cultural change follows a single, even trajectory. Yet, as discussed in Chapter 1, cultural change can be much more non-linear and exhibit periodicities and cycles with change occurring at different rates at different periods. This is exactly what Holbrook and Bidwell seem to be suggesting in their revision of Gillam's chronology. What they do not do, is explain why this happens. For this, we need to look at the broader picture. Questions of fluctuation in ceramic output in relation to the economic cycles of Roman Britain have been raised, both in regard to imports such as *terra sigillata* (Greene 1982), and, more broadly, to regional pottery traditions (Going 1992). But of particular relevance here are Going's comments on the implications of this for dating; he suggested that because of this fluctuating output, dates of vessels produced in periods of low ceramic activity will cover broader time spans than those in periods of growth (Going 1992). He suggested using a calibration curve to offset this. Using this argument to explain the breakdown of Gillam's dating for certain periods, we might suggest that the dating of Black Burnished ware vessels before AD 120 and after AD 240 is more ambiguous because their production spans are much longer than conventionally thought because of the slowness of the economy, and vice versa for those vessels produced between AD 120 and 240 in the heyday of the industry. A hypothetical calibration graph for Black Burnished ware cooking pots may be something like that shown in Figure 4.4. Two date ranges are shown, A and B; date A, conventionally dated to AD 90–110 needs to be adjusted to AD 60–110, while B, dated to AD 160–180 remains the same. Fortunately, our jar 3732 falls within the regular period of change during the peak of the industries, so its close dating can more or less be retained.

The major problem of the conventional type series in this case relates to an assumption of regular change – which clearly does not seem to happen, as stylistic change would appear to be affected by the economic cycles of ceramic production. However, there could be a further reason why chronologies break down which has more to do with the structure of type series in the first

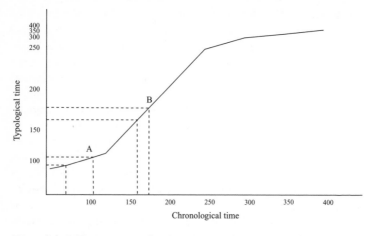

Figure 4.4 Calibration curve for the jar type series.

place; a problem of not recognizing the non-linearity or multi-temporality of stylistic change. In the case of the type series relating to jar 3732, the chronological development of the cooking pot is represented by a series of successive types, as shown in Figure 4.3. While it may be recognized that the definitions of each type can be blurry and that individual examples may not fit neatly into such classifications – or even that the types actually just represent arbitrary points on a continuum (as Gillam no doubt intended) – archaeologists still generally persist in using such classifications as heuristic devices for ordering their data. There has been varied debate on such issues in typology, especially as they relate to alternate methods of creating types, but whatever methods one uses the ultimate product is a typology or type series. However, I would suggest this very goal tends to separate unnecessarily the two aspects of time discussed in Chapter 1 – the A and B series or duration and sequence. For example, each type has duration – a period of currency, a production span; jar 3732 spans AD 120–160. But this duration is more or less independent of the duration of other types – for example, the duration of types preceding and replacing our jar type will often overlap with the beginning and end of the production cycle. This overlap is possible because each type has an autonomous duration, and is only related to other types through their sequential ordering.

The advantage of a type series where sequence and duration are related to each other and not autonomous, is that the tension between continuity and change is kept foregrounded, enabling a multi-temporal or non-linear representation of stylistic change. In Figure 4.5, the development of the cooking pot, of which our jar is an example, is shown in an alternative presentation, using just two attributes for simplicity – the rim form and the decoration on the body. A fuller chart would show many more attributes, but the key point is that different elements of the jar design will change at different rates. In this simplified example, the development of the rim clearly exhibits a very different temporal dynamic to the decoration. The advantage here is that any individual cooking pot, rather than being assigned to a 'type' can actually be compared attribute-for-attribute, to yield a date range – particularly useful, too, if one has only a part of the vessel. Our pot, for

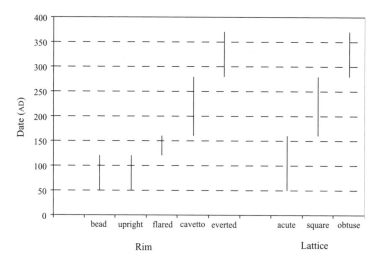

Figure 4.5 Time chart for jar attributes.

example, has a flared rim and acute lattice, and on these two attributes, can be dated to AD 120–160. If more attributes had been included in this chart, not only might it refine the dating but, more significantly, the multi-linear nature of stylistic change would be greatly enhanced, with the potential for separating larger from smaller cycles of change. For example, although the lattice design on the body shows a successive shift from acute to obtuse, on longer-term scale, the band width of the lattice as a whole changes from broad to narrow.

In this section, I have discussed many different aspects of the chronology of one object, a (typologically defined) cooking pot re-used as a cremation vessel. I discussed how it was entwined in at least five different chronological systems, and that sometimes these systems are incommensurable, which can lead to false problems caused by scales of resolution, but can also highlight real problems, caused by assumptions of regular, uni-linear change. There are many chronologies in use in archaeology, but even within one chronological system, the notion of different scales of change or resolution can be exploited productively, especially in connection to typological development. However, there is more to the temporality of this jar than simply multiple chronologies. The jar is a concrete object, an individual and unique artefact – not just an example of a type. Its very individuality is also caught up in time and, indeed, it is this individual temporality that discloses the possibility of archaeology as a temporal discipline.

The biography of jar 3732

If the attributes of jar 3732 – its rim or decoration – have specific durations of greater or shorter length, then the jar itself, as the material realization of these attributes has a much longer duration. Indeed, while it started life in a potter's workshop, somewhere in the south-east of England in the early–mid-second century AD, it is still surviving today, 1,820 years later. That is quite an age. How do we start to characterize this age, though, beyond its mere calendrical notation? What is its biography? Figure 4.6 shows the life history of this jar, punctuated by key

THE LIFE AND TIMES OF A ROMAN JAR

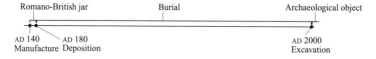

Figure 4.6 Time line for jar 3732.

changes of context; it is these changes that provide a narrative structure for relating the jar's biography, like chapters in a book. It begins, as I have already said, in a potter's workshop, where it was shaped, dried, burnished and fired before being transported to a local market where it passed on, ultimately, to its owners at the settlement mentioned at the start of this chapter. Almost everything about the appearance of the vessel was defined in this first stage of its life; everything subsequent to it left very little or no material traces on it, but slight though these traces may be, they can help us to understand its biography.

Archaeologists have developed a number of techniques for examining the use life for a range of different artefacts; in terms of ceramics, one would examine chips or scratches to indicate wear, residues to indicate possible use, and other modification features such as repair holes or graffiti. All these scars testify to the 'life experiences' of the jar, and give some idea of its biography and, thus, age profile. Jar 3732 exhibits very little identifiable wear or residues, and what attrition it has suffered could equally come from post-depositional processes as from use. We can, therefore, infer that the jar did not see excessive use between the time it was made and the time it was deposited with the cremation in the pit. Indeed, we know the jar was made some time between AD 120 and 160 and we know the cremation burial probably dates to some time between AD 140 and 180. This means the jar was, at most, 60 years old when buried, but in all likelihood, was much younger given what is known from ethnographic studies of the use life of such vessels, and the fact that it shows little sign of intensive use. Still, it could be a curated heirloom. If we could refine this chronology, the potential for exploring this question would, of course, be significant, especially in terms of the cremation ritual – what kind of 'age' do pots used in cremations exhibit? Is there a repeated pattern – are they normally 'old' or brand new? What might this say about people's attitudes to time in relation to objects in the context of burials?

These are questions that this example cannot answer, but it is conceivable that other examples may be able to tackle them. Certainly, just by asking them, we are opening up new possibilities in exploring the temporality of the jar, temporalities that people in the past may have been conscious of. Moreover, this does raise the more general question of what we might call the *age profile* of the jar; for the jar ages not simply in chronological or calendrical time as shown in Figure 4.6, but in each phase or stage of its biography it acquires a unique age profile according to its cultural context. I have just suggested ways in which we might explore the age profile of the jar as it existed during its use in the Roman period, particularly how old it was during its archaeological context of deposition. But this age is not simply a question of the number of years that have elapsed since it was made, but its 'social age'. For example, if I go out and buy two pairs of shoes, both might be brand new, but one pair may be the latest fashion while another may be in a style even my father would have worn. Some styles may be 'old', even if the object is new; the style of jar 3732 is fairly contemporary in many senses – as a type, it was made for only about 40 years. But when we consider the jar as part of a wider genealogy – most clearly expressed in the chart of Figure 4.5 – then the jar evokes a very old tradition going back to the Late Iron Age. It is not a Roman style vessel (unlike the two flagons accompanying it in the cremation burial). How much this would have been perceived by the people who used it in the past is debatable however, especially as, regionally, the style refers to a different part of England than that in which it was made or consumed. Nevertheless, we can suggest that the jar does reference a potentially deeper temporal awareness than that simply indicated by its strict chronology.

The concept of age profile thus helps us to understand the biography of the jar in a much richer way than simply as chronological aging. In strict chronological time, the jar's age is relentless and singular – it was created some time between AD 120 and 160, and has aged since then along a single time line. But because the jar has a life history, each stage in that history will incorporate its own age profile. The first major period of the jar's life encompasses the period between its production and its deposition in the cremation burial – a period of no more than 60 years. Thereafter, it enters a period of limbo – effectively, suspended animation. This is not to say it does not age in the sense of suffering slow and gradual attrition from post-depositional factors, but this is a profile we retrospectively place on the jar, after it has been excavated. Its excavation marks the start of a new period in the life history of the jar. Because of the intervening period of burial and suspension, when it was excavated in 2000 it was as if it was re-created and acquired a new profile. Indeed, just as we suggested that something very new in chronological terms might still evoke an old temporality in social terms, conversely, something that is very old chronologically, can be quite new in another sense, as not having been seen before. When archaeology first started, it unearthed many ancient objects – but while these were old, they were also quite new in the sense of not being a part of the contemporary material culture. Few people, if any, had seen prehistoric tools or Romano-British pots – or if they had, they had not been recognized as such. Indeed, it was archaeology that created the terms by which such objects could be identified.

Consider our jar. It has a generic name – 'BB2 cooking pot'. This fixes the jar within a mnemonic system, but one that was only created half a century ago. Studies of Romano-British coarse ware pottery were relatively undeveloped until the mid-twentieth century; most attention was given to fine wares, especially imports such as the bright red *terra sigillata* or samian by early archaeologists (Tyers 1996). The type 'BB2' is an acronym for 'Black Burnished ware 2' and was defined along with BB1 by the Roman ceramicist John Gillam in the late 1950s and early 1960s (Gillam 1957). Gillam revolutionized Romano-British pottery studies by making coarse wares the subject of detailed study, providing key type series for the north of England. BB1 was, and is, regarded as a coherent industry and style, emerging out of a late Iron Age ceramic tradition in the south-west of England, while BB2 is seen as an imitation of this by later factories in the South-east. Since the 1950s, BB1 has, itself, been sub-divided into at least three sub-varieties according to its source of manufacture (Farrar 1973), yet it still retains a degree of homogeneity. BB2 however, vacillates between being similarly variable to extremely heterogeneous, as the style of vessels copying BB1 can be seen to cover a much wider variety than would be conventionally classed as BB2. The use of the term BB2 to define jar 3732 is thus equivocal, hence the designation 'BB2-type', and it may be that in another 50 years' time, the classification will no longer be in use. In short, our identification of the jar incorporates the temporality of Romano-British pottery studies, and this identification must be seen as historical, not absolute. In this respect, if our jar had been excavated in 1960, it might be regarded as quite a new find – archaeologists simply were not looking for, or even interested in, these kind of vessels before, even if they did find them. It is only when a system of classification was developed that the jar starts to take on a specific meaning and, in the early days of this classification, our jar would have been quite new. Now, half a century later, it is quite an old jar, as it is easily recognizable. For the archaeologists finding this jar in 2000, it was old not simply because it was nearly 2,000 years old, but also because it was a long-recognized type.

Beyond its historical characterization within the discipline of archaeology, the classification of the jar can also be seen as a kind of mnemonic system used by archaeologists. Consider the number 3732. Archaeologists love to use numbers, they assign numbers to everything – layers, sites, artefacts, records. The number of our jar is part of a number system for all the finds recovered from one site, and each number helps to identify a unique artefact or group of finds from that site. We use numbers because we need to be able to index a whole range of different elements – this jar to this layer and feature by association to other finds in that layer or feature. Such numbers (like typologies) are effectively part of a mnemonic system, an extension of human memory that enables us to remember where and in what context an archaeological entity occurred and, thus, to investigate its relation to other entities. On a small site, we might be able to remember individual finds and features – this pit had this pot sherd in it – but this is not possible in most cases and, more significantly, it relies solely on individual memory. A number system, on the other hand, can be shared by anyone, it is an external or artificial memory system, to use the term applied to those Palaeolithic tally sticks discussed in Chapter 3. Thus, the number is indicative of a temporal strategy by archaeologists that enables them to prac-tise their discipline. Time, as the extension of archaeological memory, lies at the basis of the number 3732.

Jar 3732 now sits in a brown box, among hundreds of others in a warehouse out in the middle of nowhere. On the box, the site code and accession numbers are clearly written and should anyone care to take a look, it can be found. Yet, in many ways, the jar is sinking into oblivion again, as it did when it was first buried with the cremation nearly 2,000 years ago. As time goes by, it will be forgotten and only the echo of its existence will remain in a text such as this, and as such texts are no longer read, so the last memories of the jar will fade. This is the fate of most such arte-facts excavated – only the lucky few manage to make it into the museum case and remain on view, indeed, enter a wider public consciousness. As archaeologists, I wonder if we prefer our objects buried, dead.

To end this chapter, I want to broaden these reflections on the temporality of jar 3732 and consider, in particular, the temporal-ities of the past and the present as they are entwined within it. The connection between the past and the present would *appear to be* somehow guaranteed through the materiality of this jar. Yet, that it was made nearly 2,000 years ago, and circulated in a very different society to the one it is in today, suggests a vast chasm between us and the community who used and buried the jar. But it is a chasm that we bridge – and that, it can be suggested, we created in the first place – through the strategy of a universal historical chronology, calendrical time. That we can put the jar at one point along this continuum and ourselves, the present, at another, is a powerful way of making the connection, and even if we cannot be precise in our allocation of the jar on this timeline, the very attempt is sufficient. But the very fact that we can recognize another temporality besides chronology – its age profile as perceived by people in Roman Britain only serves to split what chronology has connected. Their experience of time and the temporality of the jar is so different from ours. Yet, from another perspective, this age profile can actually bring the past closer to us than chronology – by making the past seem *as if it were present*. By discussing the age profile of the jar, and the temporal experience of people in the past, they become almost like contemporaries, people whom we try to understand and have a dialogue with – like ethnographic subjects, not like people who died nearly 2,000 years ago. For while chronology may help to bridge the distance between then and now through an unbroken continuum, at the same time it also re-asserts the vast distance and time which has elapsed – it reasserts their *pastness*.

Of course, in many ways this is exactly the problem with 'ethnographic' narratives of the past – they deny the very thing that it is – past. Yet, there is a fundamental dilemma here, for there is a sense in which both strategies – chronology and age profiling – perform the same thing but in different ways. They mediate the problem of continuity and discontinuity between present and the past but, in doing so, they each elide a different aspect of time, which impoverishes the temporality of the object. Seeing the jar in chronological time creates continuity with the present through a single line, yet because the continuity is created though an abstraction, the experience of temporality is removed – any sense of flux, of past/present/future is replaced by earlier/later, by sequence. Conversely, viewing the jar in terms of its age profile emphasizes this experiential time, it inserts the jar into a 'present' like ours with perceptions of the past and future entwined within this present, through concepts such as 'old' or 'new'. Yet, in turning it into a 'contemporary', a living (archaeo/ethnographic) present, it denies the fact that it is a past to our present – it denies the very passage of time and change that is the hallmark of a historical science. These two temporalities are not necessarily exclusive, but they are radically different and promote different philosophies of time – what might be characterized as the A and B series, as discussed in Chapter 1. Archaeology is, perhaps, best when it draws on both strategies, but it does not necessarily have to reconcile them.

This question of two temporalities raises a number of deeper issues for archaeology – issues about how archaeology is defined by time as well as how it defines time. This is a subject I take up in the next and final chapter. However, in conclusion, it is worth asking how it is I have claimed to be talking about one object in this whole chapter – is jar 3732 a stable entity? Is it two different objects according to these two temporalities or is it the same object – and if the latter, how? Is there anything more than the coherence given by this narrative, this Chapter 4 which enabled me to talk of a stable object such as this jar – or is it simply this narrative that has guaranteed this stability? Does the jar exist – persist in any way separate from the temporality of the (meta)narrative that is Chapter 4?

5

CONCLUSIONS

Forgetting the past

Retrospect/prospect

The themes addressed in the first three chapters, and the case study in the last, are not necessarily exhaustive and are, moreover, inevitably partial. Nevertheless, I hope this book has given more than a flavour of the issues surrounding the concept of time in archaeology, and explored it in sufficient detail for the reader to have engaged with its significance. The topic of time in archaeology is both old and new – as reviewed in Chapter 1, it is clearly a central concept in archaeology, and in terms of dating and the development of chronology generally, it has been a key part of the discipline for over a century. But more reflexive and critical thinking of the concept and what it means is much more recent – indeed, Mark Leone's paper was, perhaps, the first to break new ground, and throughout the 1980s and 1990s, a slow but sure momentum has built up with discussion developing from the abstract critique of Shanks and Tilley to the concrete studies of Bradley.

To give some signposts to where I think the discussion of the topic will go in the future, I would first like to recapitulate the key themes discussed so far. This book started with the notion that it would go beyond chronology. However, throughout, I have strived to stress that archaeology needs chronology and while it might be possible to do a specific archaeological study without it, as a discipline it remains fundamentally dependent on it. The very constitution of archaeological data is entangled with chronological time. But this does not mean chronology should hold exclusivity or even primacy in this domain; chronology is a very particular conceptualization of time and there are many others. Moreover, there is the broader issue of whether archaeology is somehow defined by chronology – that is, its subject matter – an issue I take up in more detail below. However, to recap first. I argued that chronology has often provided the model for explanations of change: chronological time being singular, linear, uniform and most importantly of all, total, it has tended to similarly influence our perception of culture change. Because chronology represents time as a container for events, as something that can transcend or stand outside the specific context of events or objects, a model of history that is equally transcendent has dominated much of archaeological thought – nowhere better expressed than in evolutionism. Since the late 1980s, more particularistic historical trajectories have been argued for and, in particular, two main 'schools' have shown alternatives to the totalizing history of evolution: the *Annales* and non-linear dynamics. While both of these still rely on chronology, they do not follow its conception of time in their interpretation of the past. Critical to both approaches is that the nature of historical events is not separate from time but, rather, the two are interdependent. This is expressed through the notion of temporal scales and the idea that different events are associated with different temporal rhythms. Time is not an abstract or independent container for events but is moulded by them as much as it moulds them.

In Chapter 2, I turned my attention to the relation of time to the archaeological record, specifically questioning the conventional notion of it as something static or 'dead'. Debates between Schiffer and Binford and the 'Pompeii Premise' float over the more basic conception that the archaeological record is something that is no longer active; that somehow in becoming an archaeological record, the material remains of past events have been taken out of time and history. But this conception is solely based on an epistemological split of the archaeologist and the archaeological record which translates into a temporal schism between the present and the past. It was suggested that this schism can only be maintained because of the way time is reduced to its conception as chronology – something abstract and independent of event and context. Once it is accepted that time is interdependent with context, as argued in Chapter 1, then the separation of past and present and its role as an epistemological device sustaining the separation of object and subject, collapses.

A second issue relating to the archaeological record was its supposed similarity to the ethnographic record; this is a point that has been developed more fully under the rubric of time perspectivism and the notion that the archaeological record encompasses quite different timescales than the ethnographic record. It was argued, however, that this misrepresents the temporality of the ethnographic record as a singular present, rather than a multi-temporal field of pasts, presents and futures. This multi-temporality is well captured in the term 'palimpsest', which is not meant to be taken as a static layering of events but an ongoing process. A critique of time perspectivism was based on two key issues: first, its association between temporal scales of historical explanation and an inherently different ontology of the archaeological record. Second, a conflation of real or narrative time and chronological time in terms of temporal resolution in the archaeological record. As with the first issue, it is an adherence to chronological time that is at the root of the problem, and discussion shifted to the nature of narrative time as the primary key to moving away from the epistemology of a past–present schism or the ontology of time perspectivism.

Narrative time is something that is very subtle but still influences in a major way our perception of time in archaeology. The fact that narrative structures embody a particular view of time can both sustain conventional conceptions of time and challenge them. Most archaeological narratives are linear and represent time as chronology – a progressive movement in one direction. Evolutionary and origin stories were cited as prime examples, but even periodization can be viewed as a sedimented narrative with the same structure. Biographical narratives – of sites or artefacts – which are a new genre, to some extent retain the same form, but they do have the potential to challenge the chronological notion of time by unchaining elements of a story from a chronological frame and juxtaposing different times in a non-linear manner. Ultimately, however, the structure of narrative seems inextricably tied to chronological time and, perhaps, the most salient point is not to deny archaeological narratives a linear structure but, rather, to ensure this linearity remains open to the possibility of temporal disruptions and dislocations so the story does not have the appearance of inevitability.

One way of achieving this was explored in Chapter 3 – namely, through an investigation into past perceptions of time. Through looking at ethnographic studies of other societies' conceptions of time, some ideas of how to study time in past societies were gathered. In particular, how time perception is linked to the temporal structure of practice was a key recognition, and archaeological studies that examined such temporal structures as individual or household cycles or, more generally, the role of social memory in societal reproduction were presented. However, the link back to temporal perception was often weak or even non-existent, and discussion moved on to examine more specific studies of how past societies viewed their past. Here a rich source of examples was found that revolved around key practices such as re-use or imitation which could be interpreted as specific manifestations of past people's attitudes to *their* past. How past societies engaged with material culture that was ancient in their time becomes the key to understanding an aspect of their temporal perception of the world.

One of the major points made in this context was a cautionary note on the dangers of over-polarizing such temporal perceptions – especially from outdated social theory – such as linear/cyclical or abstract/substantial. Indeed, any interpretation that tends to fall back on the notion of chronotypes – that is, a typology of temporal perceptions – was criticized on the grounds that it limits the uniqueness and complexity of social perceptions of time, and simply fitting a prehistoric society or practice into a ready made chronotype is really to deny what is specific about that society's perception of time. Much more informative and innovative are those studies that retain unique narratives about past societies and, through an analysis of the particular practices, generate particular histories. This is not to deny the usefulness of certain generalizations and even certain broad conceptions – such as re-use/imitation, novel/old, but these are methodological tools for exploring particular stories rather than preformed genres to which the data is fitted.

There is a lot more scope for exploring time in past societies, especially how it inflects with other social practices and concepts, such as power and gender. To what extent did different sections of a prehistoric community experience time differently, and in association with what contexts? Such questions have barely been posed and, indeed, this is not surprising given the fact that time itself is such a recent topic of analysis. One can hope, however, that such issues will be addressed in the future. There is also more potential in exploring the relationship between culture change and time. Archaeologists still mostly employ flat chronological approaches to change, yet the possibility of multiple temporali-ties, analysis at many levels, remains to be developed fully, whether within existing schools such as the *Annales* or not. How this might affect how archaeology is ultimately written or taught is also a key prospect – might traditional periodization be aban-doned altogether? How would one teach prehistory without this structure? Finally, archaeological narratives can not only be written at different scales but also employing different temporal voices – this, perhaps, remains the most undeveloped of all aspects of time theory in archaeology, and one that could radically alter our perception of archaeology as a discipline concerned with the past. Ultimately, re-thinking the concept of time in archaeology should mean re-thinking the nature of archaeology as a contem-porary practice. It is this issue that I want to focus on in the remainder of this chapter.

Back to the future

If someone were to invent a time machine, would archaeology become redundant? I ask this hypothetical question because it forces us to think about the nature of archaeology in relation to time. I suppose many of us would answer in the affirmative; if we could just whiz back to the twenty-first century BC to witness a burial in prehistoric Britain, then what would be the point in spending time and effort, excavating the remains of this burial in the twenty-first century AD? After all, we would see everything that went on, all the events involved and their associated objects, many of which may have perished or been removed since. We could even interview, or at least try to communicate with, the mourners, ask them what they thought about this burial, about the deceased, why they were doing certain things and what certain objects meant. I do not deny such a scenario is highly tantalizing and even produces a kind of 'ethnographic envy' in me, but then this archaeological fantasy is, perhaps, not all it quite appears.

In the first case, being able to observe events in the past really only puts us into the same position as ethnographers and we would simply substitute one set of problems for another. All the complexities of conducting ethnographic fieldwork – of cultural translation, of communication – would face us, and we would share the same doubts and ambiguities as any ethnographer. The prehistoric society would be no more transparent to us for simply being our contemporary. This is not to deny we would not necessarily learn new things, even answer many questions that are, otherwise, forever beyond our ability to grasp. But, more seriously, this fantasy also fails to recognize that archaeology and ethnography are two very different practices, working with different problems and data. Indeed, the point about archaeology is that it engages with material culture and uses highly specialized techniques to understand it. Ethnoarchaeology or, more generally, archaeological and material culture studies of contemporary society, show that even though we can observe a society ethnographically, there is a very different story to be told by looking at it through an archaeological lens (Buchli and Lucas 2001). If a time machine was invented, perversely, I would suggest that as archaeologists, we would go back to the twenty-first century BC and only end up using just the same techniques and modes of reasoning that we would in the twenty-first century AD!

CONCLUSIONS

What does this tell us about the nature of time in relation to the practice of archaeology? In Chapter 2, I discussed the question of time perspectivism and, in particular, raised doubts over Binford's characterization of the archaeological record as distinct from the ethnographic record. Some further clarification is now needed on this problem, for what I have just said would seem to contradict this earlier stance. The characterization of the ethnographic record discussed in Chapter 2 revolved primarily around its nature as a 'living present'; Binford suggested that the archaeological record encompassed long time spans, whereas the ethnographic record was simply caught in the present moment. As I argued, this was a false representation of the present, which is, in fact, multi-temporal and encompasses multiple timescales, as demonstrated in Olivier's papers. However, this does not mean there is no difference between the ethnographic and archaeological records. The problem is, Binford presupposed the archaeological record to lie exclusively in the past – hence the privilege of retrospect. But the archaeological record is all around us, it is always in the present – sometimes buried, sometimes visible, sometimes undisturbed, sometimes a living part of our daily lives. The difference between the ethnographic and archaeological records is one of *primary orientation*; in the case of ethnography, this is to other people, in the case of archaeology, to material culture. I do not want to over-stress the role of material in the definition of disciplines or, indeed, the distinction between disciplines. Archaeology, history and ethnography all potentially overlap in their orientation to material culture, documents and people respectively.

Yet, if archaeology is primarily about material culture, it is also about time – or rather there is a distinct temporality to the material culture of archaeology in contrast to, say, ethnography or history. This temporality, however, does not reside in chronology; time as chronology plays no role whatsoever in constituting archaeology, as archaeological methods and investigation can apply to objects and contexts a few hours old just as usefully as those thousands of years old. The temporality that constitutes the nature of archaeology is quite different and one that I want to focus on in the remainder of this chapter.

Prehistory and the duality of time

That archaeology is concerned with the past would be a truism, were it not such a complex issue. For although archaeology as a discipline began by exploring the deep past of prehistory, it has, particularly since the 1960s, turned its attention to more recent periods including the present (e.g. Schiffer and Gould 1981; Buchli and Lucas 2001). But is this 'present' any less past than deep prehistory? Is it not just a contemporary past, as opposed to a historical past or prehistoric past? No matter where archaeology directs its gaze, its subject matter will always be in the past. Indeed, perhaps the very act of the gaze is what makes it past, like the stare of the Gorgon. Is an archaeology of the present, as the present, ever truly possible?

Well, in one sense all archaeology is of the present – it is situated and practised in the present, even if it is about the past. Indeed, this is the basis of the radical critique of post-processualism against an archaeology that ignores the social and political context in which archaeological knowledge is created (Shanks and Tilley 1987a). But characterized this way, ironically, there is a danger that past and present remain polarized terms, and archaeology becomes something solely contained within the present. This is certainly not the point of the post-processual critique, indeed, it has been, and is, about emphasizing the interconnection between past and present. In many ways, this issue is really about the relation between subjectivity and objectivity in relation to time or, more specifically, about how archaeology makes its object.

The phrase 'the past is a foreign country' is now so familiar it needs no explanation (Lowenthal 1985). But just as archaeology likens its object through a spatial metaphor of distant lands, so anthropology articulates its object through a temporal metaphor of another time (Fabian 1983; Thomas 1989). As Fabian has so clearly demonstrated, anthropology has traditionally constructed its object through the denial of coevalness, by which he means: 'a persistent and systematic tendency to place the referent(s) of anthropology in a time other than the present of the producer of anthropological discourse' (Fabian 1983: 31). It has done this, according to Fabian, chiefly by using different temporal tropes such as chronology, periodization and other typologies which separate the time of the subject from that of its object (e.g. primitive/modern, savage/civilized etc.; see Stahl 1993 for how this is applied in archaeology). The conceptualization of time in relation to the Other is thus something both anthropology and archaeology share, and while it is perhaps more coded in anthropology, it is, conversely, so blatant in archaeology that perhaps we miss it altogether and so have to use the spatial metaphor of foreign lands instead. Yet to do this is, perhaps, to obscure the point still further – in denying the temporal aspect to archaeology's object or Other, we are in danger of losing what is unique about archaeology by turning it into a pseudo-ethnography. The irony here is that while it is legitimate for anthropology to upbraid itself for its denial of coevalness, for archaeology to do so, is surely perverse.

No one makes this point more strongly than Murray (whose arguments we met in Chapter 2), particularly where he laments how the vastness of time, which was opened up by the discovery of the antiquity of humankind, was so quickly tamed through the application of ethnographic analogy (Murray 1993; but see Trautmann 1992). Indeed, in many ways Murray turns Fabian's argument on its head, for he suggests that if anthropology has used time to construct its object since the nineteenth century, simultaneously its object was also used to construct time. Specifically, anthropology and the ethnographic present were used to create a model of prehistoric time. I want to examine how the emergence of the idea of prehistory is closely linked to archaeology's construction of its object as the past. For, indeed, one could suggest that, in fact, all archaeology is ultimately about prehistory, even an archaeology of the contemporary past, if by prehistory we mean a specific archaeological time which its object inhabits.

When the term 'prehistory' was introduced by Daniel Wilson in *The Archaeology and Prehistoric Annals of Scotland* (1851), it took some time for it to be generally accepted, for the word implied a time in which humans lived before history, which seemed contradictory (Daniel 1962). Daniel remarks – and, of course, it is something we accept today – that history is understood as written history, and therefore prehistory is history before written records (ibid.: 10). Wilson's own text would seem to lend some support to this idea, for in his introduction he remarks on the large gap in time between the first settlement of Britain and the earliest written evidence (Wilson 1851). Daniel's book does not really pursue this much further – rather, in his account of the idea of prehistory, he launches upon a history of prehistoric research, and does everything, in fact, except look at the idea of prehistory. Why should there be a need to distinguish prehistory from history and why does this distinction fall upon the absence of written evidence?

There is much more to this than simply a question of methods. Today, we might say that the difference is not perhaps between history and prehistory but history and archaeology – i.e. the difference in data and corresponding methodology – but this is not what was said in the nineteenth century, and the legacy of this in our present use of the word prehistory is still evident. It is an interesting point that when Lubbock was writing his book *Prehistoric Times* he considered the word 'antehistory' instead of 'prehistory' (Daniel 1962: 10). He cannot have been unaware of its homophony to 'ant*i*history', which would distance this period of time even more from written history, and given the much stronger evolutionary tone of Lubbock's book compared to Wilson's this may be very revealing. The point being that prehistory was separate from history not simply because of a lack of written material – this merely signified a more fundamental schism between a present and a past history.

Prior to the adoption of the Three Age System – which Wilson's book seems to have been the first to apply to British archaeology (Trigger 1989) – there was a widespread separation of history into a Heathen and Christian period (Sklenár 1983: 88; also see Fabian 1983: 27). The use of ethnographic parallels to flesh out the Heathen period has a long history (Hodgen 1964), and is intimately linked with the rise of evolutionism. More significant, though, is the manner in which the Heathen as Other residing on the periphery of the world is projected temporally into the Other Time: prehistory (Fabian 1983; Friedman 1985). As the Heathen became the object of a scientific discipline, ethnology, it is even more distanced, and that this should carry over into archaeology was inevitable. It is interesting in this respect that Wilson laments the fact that at the time of publication, archaeology had still not been accepted as a science by the British Association, even though its close relative, ethnology was just admitted that year (Wilson 1851, preface). Wilson was very specific about aligning archaeology with the sciences and not history, indeed, the impetus for the Scandinavian developments was the need to establish the museum collections in a scientific rather than simply decorative manner (Gräslund 1987). Prehistory was a natural, not a historical science. Prehistoric time is the time before writing, and it may be no accident that writing was regarded as the defining feature of this break owing to the deeper associations between nature and speech on the one hand, and writing and culture on the other (Derrida 1976).

All this would seem to suggest that there was a major conceptual barrier between prehistory and history that required a verbal distinction. However, this needs to be set against a counter tendency that favoured continuity between prehistory and history, in the context of nationalism. In as much as archaeology was born as the twin of anthropology, it also emerged as the nation states of Europe were re-defining themselves and their identity (Diaz-Andreu and Champion 1996; Kohl and Fawcett 1995). Nationalism clearly played a major role in the rise of interest in antiquities and the use of the archaeological heritage to trace a national ancestry back into prehistory. This opposing tendency of the meaning of prehistory in the late nineteenth century – as both another time and also as continuous with history – was clearly the cause of much equivocation. For example, the Danish archaeologist Jacob Worsaae, who wrote explicitly from a nationalistic perspective, also raised the possibility that cultures and races may have existed in the past that do not exist today (Daniel 1975: 50). At the time, this was received with some horror, but during the second half of the nineteenth century, such an idea was much more acceptable. The nationalistic tendency only increased over time, especially with changes that took place in archaeological thinking at the end of the century. With the resurgence of nationalism and the development of the culture history approach, continuity between history and prehistory was increasingly stressed – in Germany where the original impetus derived, the old word for prehistory *Vorgeschichte*, was replaced by *Urgeschichte* which better expressed this continuity (Sklenár 1983: 132). Similarly, Childe in his many works emphasized the continuity between prehistory and history in economic terms (e.g. Childe 1964). This development of an archaeology that stressed continuity could be seen as a re-alignment of archaeology's Object, away from ethnography towards history.

In short, then, in the later nineteenth and early twentieth centuries, the term 'prehistory' came to encompass two opposed meanings. One was of another time – a time which resembled that of the primitives who inhabited the edges of the world and a time much closer to nature (and therefore the object of science) than history. The other meaning however was the same time as history – a time in which the ancestors of modern cultures were born and in which continuity could be traced from prehistoric to historical times. In many ways, contemporary archaeology still lives in this duality. Archaeology continues to use ethnographic analogies and evolutionary models of social organization, but similarly it continues to draw on long-term histories that connect prehistory with history. Nor are these two approaches necessarily mutually exclusive. What does this mean in terms of the archaeological construction of time?

Even if Murray is right in saying that the use of the ethnographic present to characterize prehistory denies it any reality as the *past*, I think this ignores Fabian's point that the *ethnographic* present is not the same as the *ethnographers* present – there is a denial of coevalness which is done in order to perpetuate the notion of difference and otherness. It is this trope of otherness that is so crucial in the use of ethnography in archaeology, not the fact that ethnography exists in the present. The duality of ethnographic and historical time in archaeology is employed as a strategy to sustain another, more fundamental duality, that the past is both other and the same – both discontinuous and continuous with the present. This really is the key issue here, I believe – not whether archaeology should have its own conception of time, distinct from ethnography or history. Certainly, archaeology has been complicit in a domesticating strategy towards prehistory by likening it to the ethnographic present or historical time, and Murray's critique of using ethnography to recreate archaeological time on the model of the ethnographic present, is equally applicable to the use of historical time. In either case, the past, through a distinctly archaeological conception of time, appears to have been elided. But the real problem is not so much that archaeology should use a distinct conception of time, but how the very practice of archaeology is bound up with a temporalizing process – with the creation of time itself.

Archaeology as a mode of temporalization

If archaeology employs a dual conception of time, as both ethnographic and historical, then in one sense all archaeological narratives, tacitly or explicitly, incorporate this duality. Another way of putting this is to argue that all archaeology is simultaneously both prehistory and history, that the archaeology of a Second World War bomber plane is, in a very fundamental sense, prehistoric archaeology as much as it is historical archaeology. For the distinction between prehistory and history is not so much a chronological distinction – which it can be, and is usually taken to be – but an ontological distinction. It is not something that resides in the subject matter, in periodization, but something that constitutes the very act of archaeological investigation. Indeed, archaeology creates this double temporality as it constitutes its object – through alienating the archaeological record as 'past' in one move, and then attempting to suture the split through historicizing narratives that employ devices such as chronology or origin stories. Archaeology, in defining the Second World War bomber plane *as* an archaeological site, turns it into a prehistoric artefact, even though it is also constituted as a historic artefact.

126

CONCLUSIONS

Archaeologists bring techniques in the investigation of the plane which presuppose it to be alien to us, in order than it can be returned to us in a more meaningful state than when first encountered.

Archaeology creates this process of alienation by removing an object or site from the present; it removes it from the contemporary world into another time, prehistory or 'the past', an ossified realm that is separate from the present or historic time. This can be done conceptually, but is often given material form through boundaries – fences around sites or glass cases around artefacts – to underline this separation. But there is more to this separation than simple borders; there is also the appearance of those objects and sites behind these borders. Consider the nature of archaeological exhibits in museums or heritage sites – what characterizes their presentation above all else is their completeness, their pristine appearance, as if unmarked by the passage of time. There is a deep irony in most presentations of the archaeological heritage which deny the fragmented, dirty, and decayed condition in which most archaeological remains are found. Indeed, when selecting objects for display, the more complete and best preserved items are usually chosen, they undergo conservation and cleaning while sites are landscaped, structures renovated. All of this serves to give the impression that such remains have survived more or less intact and, moreover, as representatives of the archaeological record, that all such remains are in a similar condition.

Almost shamefully, archaeologists hide away the thousands and millions of broken pottery sherds, rusting ironwork, decaying bone in boxes in storerooms and in warehouses – yet it is these remains that make up almost all of the archaeological record. It is from these objects we construct narratives of the past. Why such denial? To some extent, this is not quite true: the scrappy nature of much archaeological evidence is deployed to show how clever archaeologists are; like detectives or forensic scientists, we reconstruct past worlds from such insignificant scraps. Yet, herein lies precisely the issue: reconstitution. Their 'scrappiness' ultimately needs to be transformed, fragments made whole again – either

physically or metaphorically. And the warehouses full of fragments testify to the predominance of metaphorical reconstitution.
In publications, the best items are selected for illustration and are
even 'reconstructed' on the page as whole objects, though as data,
all objects are equal. Of course, as illustrations to our narratives,
the complete, more pristine items are much more useful in many
ways; to present information on the Bronze Age, whole pots are
better than sherds – that is, though, if you want to present the
Bronze Age 'as it was', as if it were present there in the museum,
the objects of some contemporary culture. Again, this subtle and
silent move elides the passage of time, shows the Bronze Age
as if it were a contemporary (even static) culture, not a past one.
Yet, there are cracks in this show. The objects are behind glass
cases, there are humidity controls, there is an air of fragility in
their appearance, while simultaneously there is a denial of time.
Their very fragility and restricted access suggests they are subject
to the very processes of decay and destruction that their display as
whole and pristine objects denies.

At work here is a complex tension of archaeological desire that
can be exposed in our everyday evaluation of archaeological
remains. The more complete and pristine an artefact is, the greater
our feeling of awe; this is because we recognize that the passage of
time should take its toll on objects and yet, here it is, complete
and almost as if it was made yesterday. Sites like Pompeii evoke a
similar reaction – they are rare, and yet they hold us, spellbound.
An archaeological envy surrounds the condition of archaeological
sites and finds – who would not prefer their site to look like
Pompeii, their objects like those in museum cases? The other side
of this envy is the casual relegation of many archaeological finds
and sites to the category of rubbish; this site or these finds were
'crap' – a term commonly used to evaluate the condition or scarcity
of archaeological remains. In one case, surviving the passage of
time is regarded as wonderment (Pompeii), in the other, as disap-
pointment (the 'crap' site). How can we hold such contradictory
beliefs about the temporality of archaeological remains?

That archaeological remains comprise 'rubbish' is a common
truism; by this is usually meant that what archaeologists mostly

excavate is what people deliberately did not want, or discarded –
their garbage. Of course, this is only true of certain sites and
contexts (consider burials as a counter-example), but even then,
the concept of 'rubbish' applied to such remains is by no means
unequivocal (Martin and Russell 2000). However, there is a
deeper sense in which all archaeological remains are rubbish, if we
understand this concept in broader terms. If rubbish is characterized as alienated material culture – objects that are not constituted
within a network of desires or social existence but outside the
social or cultural system, then in this sense archaeological remains
are, indeed, rubbish (Lucas 2002; Douglas 1966). Prior to, and
at the moment of, discovery, they are more or less unconstituted objects. In fact, they are not simply un-constituted but
de-constituted. This is an active if silent move performed by
archaeology in characterizing its object. Before they can become
re-constituted as specific types of things – for example, whether
a ritual deposit or as Grooved ware pottery – they are already
de-constituted as archaeological objects; as objects of prehistory,
of another time. Through their constitution as specific things,
they become historical objects (even if they are 'prehistoric' in the
conventional sense).

This characterization of archaeological remains as 'rubbish'
helps us to understand the contradictory beliefs we hold about
their temporality – between Pompeii and the 'crap' site. Pompeii
almost defies the de-constituting act that archaeology performs, it
challenges its characterization as 'rubbish', for it would seem to
spring from the ground already constituted, as a recognizable
object. Most archaeological sites are not like that; they require
work – though so, of course, does Pompeii, but in a different
sense. At the other end of the spectrum is the 'crap' site, a site
conversely, that would most seem to resist re-constitution and
remain de-constituted, remains 'rubbish'. Archaeology works on
this tension between de- and re-constituting its object, but there
will always be examples at the extremes that seem to defy this
dialectic. It is these extremes that cause us in one case to be
amazed at survival and, in another, disappointed, yet these reactions are caused by the very parameters we have created. It is

archaeology itself that establishes the conditions in which these evaluations are possible at all, through the double temporality of the prehistoric past and the historic present.

Archaeology as a mode of temporalization articulates this double temporality though a rhetoric of salvage. The concept of archaeology as rescuing or salvaging the past for the present works precisely on the faultline of destruction/survival which is so central to the de-/re-constituting performance of archaeology. The greater part of all archaeological work today falls under national cultural resource management programmes – preserving and conserving a country's heritage. Archaeologists routinely engage in what used to be termed 'rescue' fieldwork – saving archaeological remains before the threat of development that would otherwise destroy such remains. However, *all* archaeology – research or contract – might be termed 'salvage' in a broader sense. Archaeology is, in most minds, associated with ruins of one sort or another – ruined buildings, decaying structures, broken objects, all variously buried or rotting on the surface. They speak of the passage of time and, ultimately, of oblivion or forgetfulness. Archaeology as a contemporary practice is very much an act of salvaging such ruins, rescuing them from oblivion – whether they are under threat from development or not. The archaeological desire is one closely bound to issues of remembrance and forgetfulness. As part of this desire, it also deploys various strategies including conservation and, in one sense, such acts may be seen as attempts to stave off decay, to arrest, and indeed reverse, time, and restore the forgotten past to memory (Shanks 1992). Indeed, the whole project of cultural resource management can be seen in this perspective with its concerns for sustainability and the notion of heritage as a finite resource.

Conservation and preservation as strategies of cultural resource management, ironically, want to stop the clock for archaeological remains; they want to take them out of time, out of the flow of time but, in doing so, they help to create the very distance and disconnection to the present that archaeological narratives try so hard to close. We adopt such strategies because we fear their loss, the same fear that actually drives us to excavate and understand such remains in the first place. Archaeological remains incorporate a temporal dilemma: on the one hand they act as material linkages to the past, as traces of the past in the present, embodying the flow of time; but on the other hand, their very fragility forces us to try to take them out of this flow, and keep them separate from the temporality that suffuses our present existence, which includes decay and destruction. I am not sure that we in archaeology are fully aware of this dilemma and its consequences, particularly of the counter-effects of our practices. We can all see how archaeology is an exciting discipline when it is involved in discovery, in uncovering traces of the past – we can all appreciate the powerful temporality embodied in archaeological remains as a link to the past. Holding a flint tool that was made and used thousands of years ago, uncovering the remains of a house hundreds of years old; such experiences are deeply engaging. But then such experiences are usually elided in the wake of discovery, either because objects are placed as frozen fetishes in museum cases or re-buried in boxes in store rooms. The attempt to preserve what we have found, and try to fix it at the moment of discovery so it does not decay means that we approach such remains like a corpse: archaeology as autopsy.

A disjunction takes place in our attitude to the temporality of archaeological remains at the moment of discovery; on the one hand, their survival from the past to the present attests to their immersion in the flow of time, but on the other hand, their continued survival from the present into the future can only be safeguarded if we arrest this very flow and treat such objects as static, fossilized, dead things no longer subject to decay. If this is the case, then archaeology is clearly embroiled in a contradictory temporal attitude to its object which is articulated in the temporal flow from past to future. Archaeology as a mode of temporalization, thus, has a double face and, in fact, helps to fragment time as much as restore it. But should it not maintain the same attitude towards the continuation of remains into the future as it does from those in the past? Surely, if it were to do so, archaeology would double its stake in the present as a culturally viable and relevant practice, one that instead of asserting continuity with the past with one hand and then removing it with the other, would remain committed to keeping that continuity alive.

Archaeology and amnesia

It is this motivating desire of archaeology for salvage – rescue the past, preserve for the future – that is driven by the fear of loss, of forgetfulness, and which establishes the dual temporality. For something to be salvaged or rescued, it must first be lost. Archaeology defines its object first as 'lost', lost to time – it resides in another time, 'prehistory', from which it seeks to rescue it, to bring it back into history, to 'our time'. But there is an inherent paradox in this characterization which will mean that the archaeological object will always at some level remain in prehistory while enfolded within history. For the archaeological object as the 'lost' object presupposes a former connection which was never there. This can best be explained by discussing archaeology as a project of collective memory. What characterizes the nature of archaeology as a social practice of collective memory? Is it, in fact, a project defined primarily by remembrance or a project defined by forgetting? The distinction may not seem significant but it is if we consider what we conventionally mean by forgetting.

Forgetfulness is largely something we define as a lapse or failure of memory. In this conception, memory is defined by the tension between remembering and forgetting, one whereby memory is maintained and kept normal, the other whereby it fails and becomes pathological. Forgetting is a pathology of memory. If I forget where I put an important paper or letter, if I forget an appointment, if I forget an event from my past, these are all seen as pathologies (even if trivial) of memory. When I remember, I can usually find the mislaid paper, meet the appointment and confirm the past event by talking to another or consulting a diary or photograph. But how does this tension work in collective memory and the context of archaeology? Let me put it squarely. In what sense is archaeology about remembering the past – about correcting a pathology of collective memory? When we excavate a site, unearth a burial, retrieve an artefact, are we remembering in the same sense as above? What confirmation can our collective consciousness give us? Moreover, in what sense can archaeological investigation be said to be initiated by an act of forgetting in a similar sense?

The answer to all these questions would seem to be 'none'. From this, it might be argued, however, that I am stretching the analogies between personal and collective memory too far, and that is why it does not seem to make sense. But I do not think so. There is certainly a sense in which society does engage in deliberate and ongoing acts of memory maintenance or eradication; war memorials or the erasure of the traces of past atrocities are all clearly acts of social remembrance or forgetting that are similar to personal memory (see Buchli and Lucas 2001, especially part II). But archaeology would seem to be of a different order, for while war memorials commemorate events within the living memory of the population, archaeology usually commemorates a past with which no one living has any personal memory. There are exceptions, chiefly in historical archaeology or the archaeology of the present; consider, for example, the Ludlow Collective's mission for archaeology making the past, 'news' again (Ludlow Collective 2001: 96). But even granting this, something different is happening in archaeology as an act of collective memory, which is more than simply a question of the archaeological remains having contemporaneity or living memory.

This difference can be explored by comparing the strategy employed in archaeology to that in everyday life with material things, especially mementoes or souvenirs. Susan Steward has argued that we need souvenirs and mementoes to provide a tangible, physical witness to events that otherwise seem to escape materialization (Steward 1984). Moreover, she suggests that though initially such objects stand in for these immaterial events, these objects soon usurp the place of the events and become, themselves, the primary subject of a narrative. In the same way, archaeology uses the material remains or traces of the past as witnesses to past events but, in the absence of any prior memory, such traces, by default, become the subject of narrative. Archaeological remains are effectively mementoes without the memory – objects with amnesia. Here is the crux. If archaeology is about collective memory, then it is of a very special sort; about a pathology *so extreme* that we cannot even confirm that it is something we forgot. Archaeology is characterized not simply by forgetfulness but amnesia, and it is a difference in kind rather than degree. Something much deeper is at stake in archaeology as a project of collective memory, namely, a sense of our collective identity.

Consider the attempts of an amnesiac to recall who they are; they gaze at photographs, meet people from the past, and hear stories, all in the hope that it might jolt them back into remembrance or provide them with the fragments of a life that they can piece back together. These memories are who they are and the key failure here is much more fundamental than a lapse of memory – it is a lapse of temporal continuity. In many ways, the amnesiac is not even comparable to ordinary memory pathologies – it is not single events or bits of discrete information that fail to be recalled, it is a radical temporal rupture between past and present. This is precisely what characterizes archaeology. However, in archaeology we do not expect a sudden revelation or illumination once all the pieces are there (though reading some earlier archaeologists about the importance of data collection over theory one might be forgiven for thinking this!). We go on collecting the fragments and patching them together into stories, believing that our reconstructions of the past get better each day, but no one believes we will finally achieve total recall. Nevertheless, as a project, it is much more about stitching up a tear in temporal continuity than a mere lapse of memory, and is thus much more about social amnesia than social forgetting.

If collective identity is what is at stake here, what collective identity is being maintained by the project of archaeology? Eviatar Zerubavel has examined the nature of collective memory in everyday, modern social contexts and suggests that representations of time and history are closely defined by what he calls 'mnemonic communities' – groups of people who construct a temporality to sustain their group identity (Zerubavel 2003). He looked at how such communities, from nations to political parties, employ different strategies to construct their time maps, many of which are familiar to archaeologists. While his study mostly focuses on time maps used in everyday life, his notion of the mnemonic community is, nonetheless, useful when juxtaposed with the profession of archaeology. Why should we as a society or culture need the distant past, even the prehistoric past as a part of our identity? Why do we need this temporal continuity to be maintained?

Archaeology, of course, has always been closely tied to nationalism and the formation of nation states, whether it is explicitly used to create origin stories or not (Diaz-Andreu and Champion 1996; Kohl and Fawcett 1995). Archaeology as the invention of traditions is undoubtedly a major factor. But archaeology has always also been a Modernist project, one that investigates pasts beyond national frontiers, as the science of the history of humankind. For this to be successful, it requires demonstrating continuity in the identity of its subject – humanity – across cultures and into the past; it also requires a continuity in time-consciousness for all human societies, past or present (Habermas 1985). When archaeology was born and scientists were faced with the vast time of prehistory, it challenged the very nature of humanity as they saw it. The radical discontinuity that archaeologists faced in the context of prehistory (and the radical discontinuity that anthropologists faced in the context of Other cultures) was closed through a narrative of evolutionism and the universal time of chronology, as discussed above.

The problem with this vision of archaeology as part of Modernity and the project of humanism lies in its politics of time. If archaeology is seen as the guardian of our time-consciousness, maintaining the temporal continuity or link with the past of humanity, what implications does this have for archaeology vis-à-vis other histories, other strategies of cultural remembrance? The question is whether this concept of time-consciousness does not claim some special and universal status, for its totalizing vision would seem to erase or denigrate other claims to the past. Archaeology is part of the hegemony of a Western discourse on history, a scientific colonialism, a *white mythology* (Young 1990). Archaeologists encounter this question of alternative histories all the time, whether it is Australian Aboriginal accounts of the past or New Age Druids, and it needs to reconcile such competing claims to the past. Such claims often seem very local and even parochial against the archaeologist's agenda but, nevertheless, they do question the universal status of archaeology. But, more radically, they might also question the very basis of the archaeo-logical record as a forgotten past that underlies everything we do as archaeologists – from salvage to conservation. Is it possible to re-think the nature of time, the nature of temporalization that archaeology creates and sustains, or is archaeology, in fact, defined by this temporality as much as it defines it? Fittingly, perhaps, only time will tell.

BIBLIOGRAPHY

Adam, B. (1990) *Time and Social Theory*, Cambridge: Polity Press.

Aitken, M.J. (1990) *Science-based Dating in Archaeology*, London: Longman.

Aldred, O. (2002) *Historic Landscape Characterisation: Taking Stock of the Methodology*, London/Taunton: English Heritage/Somerset County Council.

Almgren, B. (1995) 'The development of the typological theory in connection with the Exhibition in the Museum of National Antiquities in Stockholm', in Astrom, P. (ed.), *Oscar Montelius. 150 years*, Stockholm: Kungl Vitterhets Historie och Antikvilets Akademien.

Althusser, L. (1969) *For Marx*, London: Allen Lane.

Appadurai, A. (ed.) (1986) *The Social Life of Things*, Cambridge: Cambridge University Press.

Arden-Close, C.F. (1951) 'Time and memory', in Grimes, W.F. (ed.), *Aspects of Archaeology in Britain and Beyond*, London: H.W. Edwards.

Aristotle (1952) *Physics*, Chicago: University of Chicago Press.

Augustine (1961) *Confessions*, Harmondsworth: Penguin.

Bailey, D.W. (1993) 'Chronotypic tension in Bulgarian prehistory: 6500–3500 BC', *World Archaeology*, 25: 204–22.

Bailey, G. (1981) 'Concepts, time scales and explanations in economic prehistory', in Sheridan, A. and Bailey, G.N. (eds), *Economic Archaeology*, Oxford: British Archaeological Reports.

Bailey, G.N. (1983) 'Concepts of time in Quaternary prehistory', *Annual Review of Anthropology*, 12: 165–92.

Bailey, G.N. (1987) 'Breaking the time barrier', *Archaeological Review from Cambridge*, 6: 5–20.

Barnes, G. (1990) 'The "idea of prehistory" in Japan', *Antiquity*, 64: 929–40.

Barrett, J.C. (1988) 'Fields of discourse. Reconstituting a social archaeology', *Critique of Anthropology*, 7: 5–16.

Bender, B. (1998) *Stonehenge*, Oxford: Berg.

Bender, J. and Wellberg, D. (eds) (1991) *Chronotypes. The Construction of Time*, Stanford, CA: Stanford University Press.

Bergson, H. (1910) *Time and Free Will. An Essay on the Immediate Data of Consciousness*, London: Macmillan.

137

Binford, L. (1981) 'Behavioural archaeology and the Pompeii premise', *Journal of Anthropological Research*, 37: 195–208.

Binford, L. (1986) 'In pursuit of the future', in Meltzer, D.J., Fowler, D.D. and Sabloff, J.A. (eds), *American Archaeology Past and Future*, London: Smithsonian Institute Press.

Bintliff, J. (ed.) (1991) *The Annales School and Archaeology*, Leicester: Leicester University Press.

Bloch, M. (1954) *The Historian's Craft*, Manchester: Manchester University Press.

Bloch, M. (1977) 'The past and the present in the present', *Man*, 12: 278–92.

Bohannan, P. (1953) 'Concepts of time among the Tiv of Nigeria', *Southwestern Journal of Anthropology*, IX: 251–62.

Borić (2003) '"Deep time" metaphor: mnemonic and apotropaic practices at Lepenski Vir', *Journal of Social Archaeology*, 3: 46–74.

Bradley, R. (2002) *The Past in Prehistoric Societies*, London: Routledge.

Braudel, F. (1972) *The Mediterranean and the Mediterranean World at the Time of Philip II*, London: Collins.

Braudel, F. (1980) *On History*, London: Weidenfeld & Nicolson.

Brooks, R.L. (1982) 'Events in the archaeological context and archaeological explanation', *Current Anthropology*, 23: 67–75.

Buchli, V. and Lucas, G. (eds) (2001) *Archaeologies of the Contemporary Past*, London: Routledge.

Burkitt, M. and Childe, V.G. (1932) 'A chronological table of prehistory', *Antiquity*, 6: 185–205.

Carver, M. (1990) 'Digging for data: archaeological approaches to data definition, acquisition and analysis', in Francovich, R. and Manacorda, D. (eds), *Lo scavo archeologico: dalla diagnosi all'edizione*, Florence: All'Insegna del Giglio SAS.

Childe, V.G. (1935) 'Changing methods and aims in prehistory', *Proceedings of the Prehistoric Society*, 1: 1–15.

Childe, V.G. (1951) *Social Evolution*, London: Watts & Co.

Childe, V.G. (1956) *Piecing Together the Past*, London: Routledge & Kegan Paul.

Childe, V.G. (1957) 'Retrospect', *Antiquity*, 32: 69–74.

Childe, V.G. (1964) *What Happened in History*, Harmondsworth: Penguin.

Cipolla, C. (1967) *Clocks and Culture*, London: Collins.

Clarke, D.L. (ed.) (1977) *Spatial Archaeology*, New York: Academic Press.

Cobb, C. (1991) 'Social reproduction and the Long Durée in the Prehistory of the Midcontinental United States', in Preucel, R. (ed.), *Processual and Postprocessual Archaeologies: Multiple Ways of Knowing the Past*, Carbondale, IL: Southern Illinois University Press.

BIBLIOGRAPHY

Collingwood, R.G. (1927) 'Oswald Spengler and the theory of historical cycles', *Antiquity*, 1: 311–25.

Colman, S., Pierce, K. and Birkeland, P. (1987) 'Suggested terminology for Quaternary dating methods', *Quaternary Research*, 28: 314–19.

Conkey, M. and Williams, S.H. (1991) 'Original narratives. The political economy of gender in archaeology', in di Leonardo, M. (ed.), *Gender at the Crossroads of Knowledge*, Berkeley, CA: University of California Press.

Connerton, P. (1989) *How Societies Remember*, Cambridge: Cambridge University Press.

Dalland, M. (1984) 'A procedure for use in stratigraphic analysis', *Scottish Archaeological Review*, 3: 116–27.

Daniel, G. (1962) *The Idea of Prehistory*, Harmondsworth: Penguin.

Daniel, G. (1975) *150 Years of Archaeology*, London: Duckworth.

d'Errico, F. (1998) 'Palaeolithic origins of artificial memory systems: an evolutionary perspective', in Renfrew, C. and Scarre, C. (eds), *Cognition and Material Culture: The Archaeology of Symbolic Storage*, Cambridge: Cambridge University Press.

Derrida, J. (1976) *Of Grammatology*, Baltimore, MD: Johns Hopkins University Press.

Diaz-Andreu, M. and Champion, T. (eds) (1996) *Nationalism and Archaeology*, London: UCL Press.

Dietler, M. and Herbich, I. (1993) 'Living on Luo time: reckoning, sequence, duration, history and biography in a rural African society', *World Archaeology*, 25: 248–60.

Douglas, M. (1966) *Purity and Danger*, London: Routledge & Kegan Paul.

Durkheim, E. (1915) *Elementary Forms of Religious Life*, London: Allen Unwin.

Durrell, L. (1957) *Bitter Lemons*, London: Faber & Faber.

Evans-Pritchard, E. (1939) 'Nuer time-reckoning', *Africa*, 12: 189–216.

Evans-Pritchard, E. (1940) *The Nuer*, Oxford: Clarendon.

Fabian, J. (1983) *Time and the Other*, New York: Columbia University Press.

Farrar, R.A.H. (1973) 'The techniques and sources of Romano-British black burnished ware', in Detsicas, A.P. (ed.), *Current Research in Romano-British Pottery*, London: Council for British Archaeology.

Farrar, R.A.H. (1981) 'The first Darfield hoard and the dating of Black Burnished ware', in Anderson, A.C. and Anderson, A.S. (eds), *Roman Pottery Research in Britain and Northwest Europe*, Oxford: BAR.

Fletcher, R. (1992) 'Time persectivism, Annales and archaeology', in Knapp, B. (ed.), *Archaeology, Annales and Ethnohistory*, Cambridge: Cambridge University Press.

Forty, A. and Küchler, S. (eds) (1999) *The Art of Forgetting*, Oxford: Berg.

Friedman, J. (1982) 'Catastrophe and continuity in social evolution', in Renfrew, C., Rowlands, M. and Seagrave, B.A. (eds), *Theory and Explanation in Archaeology*, London: Academic Press.

Friedman, J. (1985) 'Our time, their time, world time: the transformation of temporal modes', *Ethnos*, 50: 168–83.

Geertz, C. (1973) 'Person, time and conduct in Bali', in Geertz, C. (ed.), *The Interpretation of Cultures*, New York: Basic Books.

Geertz, C. (1984) 'Anti anti-relativism', *American Anthropologist*, 86: 263–78.

Gell, A. (1992) *The Anthropology of Time. Cultural Constructions of Temporal Maps and Images*, Oxford: Berg.

Gerritsen, F. (1999) 'To build and to abandon. The cultural biography of late prehistoric houses and farmsteads in the southern Netherlands', *Archaeological Dialogues*, 6: 78–97.

Gillam, J.P. (1957) 'Types of Roman coarse pottery in northern Britain', *Archaeologia Aeliana*, 35: 180–251.

Gillam, J.P. (1976) 'Coarse Fumed Ware in north Britain and beyond', *Glasgow Archaeological Journal*, 4: 57–80.

Going, C. (1992) 'Economic "long waves" in the Roman period? A reconnaissance of the Romano-British ceramic evidence', *Oxford Journal of Archaeology*, 11: 93–117.

Goodman, M. (1999) 'Temporalities of prehistoric life: household development and community continuity', in Bruck, J. and Goodman, M. (eds), *Making Places in the Prehistoric World. Themes in Settlement Archaeology*, London: University College London Press.

Goody, J. (ed.) (1958) *The Developmental Cycle in Domestic Groups*, Cambridge: Cambridge University Press.

Gosden, C. (1994) *Time and Social Being*, London: Routledge.

Gosden, C. and Lock, G. (1998) 'Prehistoric histories', *World Archaeology*, 30: 2–12.

Gräslund, B. (1987) *The Birth of Prehistoric Chronology*, Cambridge: Cambridge University Press.

Greene, K. (1982) 'Terra sigillata: imitations and alternatives', *Rei Cretariae Romanae Fautorum Acta*, XXI/XXII: 71–8.

Gurevich, A. (1995) 'The French historical revolution. The Annales School', in Hodder, I., Shanks, M., Alexandri, A., Buchli, V., Carmen, J., Last, J. and Lucas, G. (eds), *Interpreting Archaeology: Finding Meaning in the Past*, London: Routledge.

Gurevich, G. (1964) *The Spectrum of Social Time*, Dordrecht: Reidel.

Habermas, J. (1985) *The Philosophical Discourse of Modernity*, Cambridge: Polity Press.

Halbwachs, M. (1992) *On Collective Memory*, Chicago: Chicago University Press.

Harkin, M. (1988) 'History, narrative and temporality. Examples from the northwest coast', *Ethnohistory*, 35: 99–130.

Harris, D. (1996) "Introduction", in Harris, D. (ed.) *The Origins and Spread of Agriculture and Pastoralism in Eurasia*, London: UCL Press.

Harris, E.C. (1989) *Principles of Archaeological Stratigraphy*, London: Academic Press.

Harris, E.C. (1991) 'Interfaces in archaeological stratigraphy', in Harris, E.C. (ed.), *Practices of Archaeological Stratigraphy*, London: Academic Press.

Hill, J.D. (ed.) (1988) *Rethinking History and Myth. Indigenous South American Perspectives of the Past*, Chicago: University of Illinois Press.

Hobsbawm, E. and Ranger, T. (eds) (1983) *The Invention of Tradition*, Cambridge: Cambridge University Press.

Hodder, I. (ed.) (1978) *The Spatial Organization of Culture*, London: Duckworth.

Hodder, I. (1985) 'Post-processual archaeology', *Advances in Archaeological Method and Theory*, 8: 1–26.

Hodder, I. (ed.) (1987) *Archaeology as Long-term History*, Cambridge: Cambridge University Press.

Hodder, I. (1993) 'The narrative and rhetoric of material culture sequences', *World Archaeology*, 25: 268–82.

Hodder, I. (1995) 'Material culture in time', in Hodder, I., Shanks, M. Alexandri, A., Buchli, V., Carmen, J., Last, J. and Lucas, G. (eds), *Interpreting Archaeology: Finding Meaning in the Past*, London: Routledge.

Hodder, I. (1999) *The Archaeological Process*, Oxford: Blackwell.

Hodder, I. and Orton, C. (1976) *Spatial Analysis in Archaeology*, Cambridge: Cambridge University Press.

Hodgen, M.T. (1964) *Early Anthropology in the Sixteenth and Seventeenth Centuries*, Philadelphia: University of Pennsylvania Press.

Holbrook, N. and Bidwell, P. (eds) (1991) *Roman Finds from Exeter*, Exeter: University of Exeter Press.

Hollis, M. and Lukes, S. (eds) (1982) *Rationality and Relativism*, Oxford: Blackwell.

Holtorf, C. (1996) 'Towards a chronology of megaliths: understanding monumental time and cultural memory', *Journal of European Archaeology*, 4: 119–52.

Holtorf, C. (1998) 'The life history of megaliths in Mecklenburg-Vorpommern (Germany)', *World Archaeology*, 30: 23–38.

Holtorf, C. (2002a) 'Excavations at Monte da Igreja near Évora (Portugal). From the life-history of a monument to re-uses of ancient objects', *Journal of Iberian Archaeology*, 4: 177–201.

Holtorf, C. (2002b) 'Notes on the life history of a pot sherd', *Journal of Material Culture*, 7: 49–71.

BIBLIOGRAPHY

Horst, K. (1954) 'Über das Verhältnis des schriftlosen frühgechichtlichen Menschen zu seiner Geschichte', *Sociologus*, 4: 9–22.

Husserl, E. (1966) *The Phenomenology of Internal Time-Consciousness*, Bloomington, IN: Indiana University Press.

Johnson, A. and Earle, T. (1987) *The Evolution of Human Societies*, Stanford: Stanford University Press.

Joyce, R. (2002) *The Languages of Archaeology*, Oxford: Blackwell.

Karlsson, H. (ed.) (2001a) *It's About Time. The Concept of Time in Archaeology*, Goteborg: Bricoleur Press.

Karlsson, H. (2001b) 'Time for an archaeological "time out"?' in Karlsson, H. (ed.), *It's About Time. The Concept of Time in Archaeology*, Goteborg: Bricoleur Press.

Kenyon, K. (1953) *Beginning in Archaeology*, London: Phoenix House.

Kertzer, D.I. and Keith, J. (eds) (1984) *Age and Anthropological Theory*, Ithaca, NY: Cornell University Press.

Knapp, B. (ed.) (1992) *Archaeology, Annales and Ethnohistory*, Cambridge: Cambridge University Press.

Kohl, P. and Fawcett, C. (eds) (1995) *Nationalism, Politics and the Practice of Archaeology*, London: Routledge.

Kovacik, J. (1998) 'Collective memory and pueblo space', *Norwegian Archaeological Review*, 31: 141–52.

Küchler, S. (1987) 'Malangan: art and memory in a Melanesian society', *Man*, 22: 238–55.

Landes, D.S. (1983) *Revolution in Time: Clocks and the Making of the Modern World*, Cambridge, MA: Belknap Press.

Lane, P. (1987) 'Reordering residues of the past', in Hodder, I. (ed.), *Archeology as Long-term History*, Cambridge: Cambridge University Press.

Last, J. (1995) 'The nature of history', in Hodder, I., Shanks, M., Alexandri, A., Buchli, V., Carmen, J., Last, J. and Lucas, G. (eds), *Interpreting Archaeology: Finding Meaning in the Past*, London: Routledge.

Latour, B. (1999) *Pandora's Hope. Essays on the Reality of Science Studies*, Cambridge, MA: Harvard University Press.

Leach, E. (1961) 'Two essays concerning the symbolic representation of time', in Leach, E. (ed.), *Rethinking Anthropology*, London: London School of Economics.

Legge, A., Williams, J. and Williams, P. (2000) 'Lambs to the slaughter: sacrifice at two Roman temples in southern England', in Rowley-Conwy, P. (ed.), *Animals' Bones, Human Societies*, Oxford: Oxbow.

Le Goff, J. (1980) *Time, Work and Culture in the Middle Ages*, Chicago: University of Chicago Press.

Lemonnier, P. (ed.) (1993) *Technological Choices. Transformations in Material Culture Since the Neolithic*, London: Routledge.

BIBLIOGRAPHY

Leone, M.P. (1978) 'Time in American archaeology', in Redman, C. (ed.), *Social Archaeology: Beyond Subsistence and Dating*, London: Academic Press.

Lévi-Strauss, C. (1963) *Structural Anthropology*, Harmondsworth: Penguin.

Lévi-Strauss, C. (1966) *The Savage Mind*, London: Weidenfeld & Nicolson.

Lillios, K.T. (2003) 'Creating memory in prehistory: the engraved slate plaques of southwest Iberia', in van Dyke, R. and Alcock, S.E. (eds), *Archaeologies of Memory*, Oxford: Blackwell.

Lowenthal, D. (1985) *The Past is a Foreign Country*, Cambridge: Cambridge University Press.

Lucas, G. (1995) 'The changing face of time: English domestic clocks from the seventeenth to nineteenth century', *Journal of Design History*, 8: 1–9.

Lucas, G. (1997) 'Forgetting the Past', *Anthropology Today*, 13: 8–14.

Lucas, G. (2001) *Critical Approaches to Fieldwork. Contemporary and Historical Archaeological Practice*, London: Routledge.

Lucas, G. (2002) 'Disposability and dispossession in the twentieth century', *Journal of Material Culture*, 7: 5–22.

Lucas, G. and Whittaker, P. (2001) 'The Roman settlement at Vicars Farm', Cambridge Archaeological Unit.

Ludlow Collective, T. (2001) 'Archaeology of the Colorado Coal Field War 1913–1914', in Buchli, V. and Lucas, G. (eds), *Archaeologies of the Contemporary Past*, London: Routledge.

McCracken, C. (1990) *Culture and Consumption*, Bloomington, IN: University of Indiana Press.

McGlade, J. (1987) 'Chronos and the oracle: some thoughts on time, time scales and simulation', *Archaeological Review from Cambridge*, 6: 21–31.

McGlade, J. (1997) 'The limits of social control: coherence and chaos in a prestige goods economy', in van der Leeuw, S. and McGlade, J. (eds), *Time, Process and Structured Transformation in Archaeology*, London: Routledge.

McGlade, J. (1999) 'The times of history: archaeology, narrative and non-linear causality', in Murray, T. (ed.), *Time and Archaeology*, London: Routledge.

McGuire, R.H. (1992) *A Marxist Archaeology*, San Diego: Academic Press.

McKendrick, N., Brewer, J. and Plumb, J.H. (eds) (1982) *The Birth of Consumer Society: The Commercialisation of Eighteenth Century England*, Bloomington, IN: University of Indiana Press.

Mackie, E. (1988) 'Investigating the prehistoric solar calendar', in Ruggles, C. (ed.), *Records in Stone. Papers in Memory of Alexander Thom*, Cambridge: Cambridge University Press.

McTaggart (1908) 'The unreality of time', *Mind*, XVII: 457–74.

Marquardt, W.H. (1978) 'Advances in archaeological seriation', *Advances in Archaeological Method and Theory*, 1: 257–314.

BIBLIOGRAPHY

Marshack, A. (1972) *The Roots of Civilization*, London: Weidenfeld & Nicolson.

Martin, A.S. (1989) 'The role of pewter as missing artifact: consumer attitudes toward tablewares in late 18th century Virginia', *Historical Archaeology*, 23: 1–27.

Martin, L. and Russell, N. (2000) 'Trashing rubbish', in Hodder, I. (ed.), *Towards Reflexive Method in Archaeology: The Example at Catalhoyuk*, Cambridge: Cambridge University Press.

Mellor, D.H. (1981) *Real Time*, Cambridge: Cambridge University Press.

Michell, J. (1977) *A Little History of Astro-archaeology. Stages in the Transformation of a Heresy*, London: Thames & Hudson.

Millett, M. (1987) 'A question of time? Aspects of the future of pottery studies', *Bulletin of the Institute of Archaeology*, 24: 99–108.

Mithen, S. (1992) *The Prehistory of Mind. The Cognitive Origins of Art and Science*, New York: Thames & Hudson.

Mizoguchi, K. (1993) 'Time in the reproduction of mortuary practices', *World Archaeology*, 25: 223–35.

Moore, H. (1995) 'The problem of origins. Poststructuralism and beyond', in Hodder, I., Shanks, M., Alexandri, A., Buchli, V., Carmen, J., Last, J. and Lucas, G. (eds), *Interpreting Archaeology. Finding Meaning in the Past*, London: Routledge.

Munn, N.D. (1992) 'The cultural anthropology of time: a critical essay', *Annual Review of Anthropology*, 21: 93–123.

Murray, T. (1993) 'Archaeology and the threat of the past: Sir Henry Rider Haggard and the acquisition of time', *World Archaeology*, 25: 175–86.

Murray, T. (1997) 'Dynamic modelling and new social theory of the mid- to long term', in van der Leeuw, S. and McGlade, J. (eds), *Time, Process and Structured Transformation in Archaeology*, London: Routledge.

Murray, T. (ed.) (1999a) *Time and Archaeology*, London: Routledge.

Murray, T. (1999b) 'A return to the "Pompeii premise"', in Murray, T. (ed.), *Time and Archaeology*, London: Routledge.

Nilsson, M.P. (1920) *Primitive Time-Reckoning*, Lund: Gleerup.

North, J.D. (1975) 'Monasticism and the first clocks', in Fraser, J.T. and Lawrence, N. (eds), *The Study of Time*, New York: Springer Verlag.

O'Kelly, M.J. (1982) *Newgrange, Archeology, Art and Legend*, London: Thames & Hudson

Olivier, L. (1999) 'The Hochdorf "princely" grave and the question of the nature of archaeological funerary assemblages', in Murray, T. (ed.), *Time and Archaeology*, London: Routledge.

Olivier, L. (2001) 'Duration, memory and the nature of the archaeological record', in Karlsson, H. (ed.), *It's About Time. The Concept of Time in Archaeology*, Goteborg: Bricoleur Press.

Patrik, L. (1985) 'Is there an archaeological record?', *Advances in Archaeological Method and Theory*, 8: 27–62.

Petrie, W.M.F. (1899) 'Sequences in prehistoric remains', *Journal of the Anthropological Institute*, XXIX: 295–301.

Piggott, S. (1959) *Approach to Archaeology*, Harmondsworth: Penguin.

Pitts, M. and Roberts, M. (1998) *Fairweather Eden*, Harmondsworth: Penguin.

Pluciennik, M. (1999) 'Archaeological narratives and other ways of telling', *Current Anthropology*, 40: 653–78.

Pocock, D.F. (1964) 'The anthropology of time-reckoning', *Contributions to Indian Sociology*, 7: 18–24.

Prigogine, I. and Stengers, I. (1984) *Order out of Chaos: Man's New Dialogue with Nature*. London: Fontana Paperbacks.

Ramenofsky, A. (1998) 'The illusion of time', in Ramenofsky, A. and Steffen, A. (eds), *Unit Issues in Archaeology. Measuring Time, Space and Material*, Salt Lake City, UT: University of Utah Press.

Renfrew, C. (1978) *Before Civilization*, Harmondsworth: Penguin.

Renfrew, C. and Cooke, K.L. (eds) (1979) *Transformations. Mathematical Approaches to Culture Change*, London: Academic Press.

Richardson, J. and Kroeber, A.L. (1952) 'Three centuries of women's dress fashions: a quantitative analysis', in Kroeber, A.L. (ed.), *The Nature of Culture*, Chicago: University of Chicago Press.

Ricoeur, P. (1988) *Time and Narrative*, Chicago: University of Chicago Press.

Rowlands, M. (1993) 'The role of memory in the transmission of culture', *World Archaeology*, 25: 141–51.

Ruggles, C. (ed.) (1988) *Records in Stone. Papers in Memory of Alexander Thom*, Cambridge: Cambridge University Press.

Sahlins, M. (1985) *Islands of History*, Chicago: University of Chicago Press.

Sahlins, M. and Service, E. (1960) *Evolution and Culture*, Ann Arbor, MI: University of Michigan Press.

Schiffer, M.B. (1972) 'Behavioural archaeology', *American Antiquity*, 37: 156–65.

Schiffer, M.B. (1976) *Behavioural Archaeology*, New York: Academic Press.

Schiffer, M.B. (1987) *Formation Processes of the Archaeological Record*, Albuquerque, NM: University of New Mexico Press.

Schiffer, M.B. and Gould, R.A. (eds) (1981) *Modern Material Culture. The Archaeology of Us*, New York: Academic Press.

Schiffer, M.B. and Skibo, J.M. (1997) 'The explanation of artefact variability', *American Antiquity*, 62: 27–50.

Shanks, M. (1992) *Experiencing Archaeology*, London: Routledge.

Shanks, M. and Tilley, C. (1987a) 'Abstract and substantial time', *Archaeological Review from Cambridge*, 6: 32–41.

Shanks, M. and Tilley, C. (1987b) *Re-Constructing Archaeology*, Cambridge: Cambridge University Press.

Shennan, S. (1975) 'The social organization at Branc', *Antiquity*, 49: 279–88.

Shennan, S. (1993) 'After social evolution: a new archaeological agenda?', in Yoffee, N. and Sherrat, A. (eds), *Archaeological Theory: Who Sets the Agenda?*, Cambridge: Cambridge University Press.

Sherrat, A. (1995) 'Reviving the grand narrative: archaeology and long-term change', *Journal of European Archaeology*, 3: 1–32.

Sinclair, A. (1987) 'Time and class: social aspects of time in 17th and 18th century England', *Archaeological Review from Cambridge*, 6: 62–74.

Sklenár, K. (1983) *Archaeology in Central Europe: The First 500 Years*, Leicester: Leicester University Press.

Sofaer Deverenski, J. (ed.) (2000) *Children and Material Culture*, London: Routledge.

Squair, R. (1994) 'Time and the privilege of retrospect', in Mackenzie, I.M. (ed.), *Archaeological Theory: Progress or Posture?*, Aldershot: Avebury.

Stahl, A. (1993) 'Concepts of time and approaches to analogical reasoning in historical perspective', *American Antiquity*, 58: 235–60.

Steward, S. (1984) *On Longing: Narratives of the Miniature, the Gigantic, the Souvenir, the Collection*, Baltimore, MD: Johns Hopkins University Press.

Tarlow, S. (1999) *Bereavement and Commemoration. An Archaeology of Mortality*, Oxford: Blackwell.

Thom, A. (1967) *Megalithic Sites in Britain*, Oxford: Clarendon Press.

Thom, A. and Thom, A.S. (1978) *Megalithic Remains in Britain and Brittany*, Oxford: Clarendon Press.

Thom, S. (1975) *Structural Stability and Morphogenesis*, Reading, MA: Benjamin Cummings Publishing.

Thomas, J. (1994) 'Discourse, totalization and "the Neolithic"', in Tilley, C. (ed.), *Interpretive Archaeologies*, Oxford: Berg.

Thomas, J. (1996) *Time, Culture and Identity. An Interpretive Archaeology*, London: Routledge.

Thomas, N. (1989) *Out of Time. History and Evolution in Anthropological Discourse*, Cambridge: Cambridge University Press.

Thompson, E.P. (1967) 'Time, work-discipline and industrial capitalism', *Past and Present*, 38: 56–97.

Thorpe, I.J. (1983) 'Prehistoric British astronomy – towards a social context', *Scottish Archaeological Review*, 2: 2–13.

Tiles, M. (1986) 'Mathesis and the masculine birth of time', *International Studies in the Philosophy of Science*, 1: 16–35.

Tourtellot, G. (1988) 'Developmental cycles of households and houses at Seibal', in Wilk, R. and Ashmore, W. (eds), *Household and Community in the Mesoamerican Past*, Albuquerque, NM: University of New Mexico Press.

BIBLIOGRAPHY

Trautmann, T.R. (1992) 'The revolution in ethnological time', *Man*, 27: 379–97.

Trigger, B. (1989) *A History of Archaeological Thought*, Cambridge: Cambridge University Press.

Tringham, R. (1991) 'Households with faces: the challenge of gender in prehistoric architectural remains', in Gero, J. and Conkey, M. (eds), *Engendering Archaeology*, Oxford: Blackwell.

Turton, D. and Ruggles, C. (1978) 'Agreeing to disagree: the measurement of duration in a southwestern Ethiopian community', *Current Anthropology*, 19: 585–600.

Tyers, P. (1996) *Roman Pottery in Britain*, London: Batsford.

van der Leeuw, S. (1993) 'Giving the potter a choice', in Lemonnier, P. (ed.), *Technological Choices*, London: Routledge.

van der Leeuw, S. and McGlade, J. (1997) 'Introduction: archaeology and non-linear dynamics – new approaches to long-term change', in van der Leeuw, S. and McGlade, J. (eds), *Time, Process and Structured Transformation in Archaeology*, London: Routledge.

van Dyke, R. (2003) 'Memory and the construction of Chacoan society', in van Dyke, R. and Alcock, S.E. (eds), *Archaeologies of Memory*, Oxford: Blackwell.

van Dyke, R. and Alcock, S.E. (eds) (2003) *Archaeologies of Memory*, Oxford: Blackwell.

Wheeler, R.E.M. (1954) *Archaeology from the Earth*, Oxford: Clarendon Press.

Williams, H. (1998) 'Monuments and the past in early Anglo-Saxon England', *World Archaeology*, 30: 90–108.

Wilson, D. (1851) *The Archaeology and Prehistoric Annals of Scotland*, Edinburgh: Sutherland and Knox.

Winter, J. (1995) *Sites of Memory, Sites of Mourning. The Great War in European Cultural History*, Cambridge: Cambridge University Press.

Wolf, E. (1982) *Europe and the People Without History*, Berkeley, CA: University of California Press.

Young, R. (1990) *White Mythologies. Writing History and the West*, London: Routledge.

Zerubavel, E. (1981) *Hidden Rhythms. Schedules and Calendars of Social Life*, Chicago: Chicago University Press.

Zerubavel, E. (2003) *Time Maps. Collective Memory and the Social Shape of the Past*, Chicago: University of Chicago Press.

Zeuner, F.E. (1946) *Dating the Past: An Introduction to Geochronology*, London: Methuen.

INDEX

INDEX

INDEX